Belmire's
667-7775
LOVELAND, COLORADO

D1595723

THE DANDIE DINMONT TERRIER

THE DANDIE DINMONT TERRIER

Giving the origin and history of the breed, its show career, its points and breeding

JOHN F. GORDON

JOHN GIFFORD LTD
LONDON

Originally published 1959 by Nicholson and Watson.
This revised edition, with many new illustrations
first published 1972 by John Gifford Ltd.

ISBN 0 7071 0303 7

*This book has been set in Garamond type, printed in Great Britain
by Cox & Wyman Ltd., London, Fakenham and Reading*

NETTIE LASS

We ha'e a Dandie we ca' Nette,
Her nose is black as polished jet;
Her tappin's white as driven snaw,
An' denkit off she looks fu' braw.

She'd play for 'oors wi' oor wee lad,
When he fell ill she fell fu' sad;
Just mounged aboot, an' wadna eat,
E'en dainty morsels were nae treat.

But when Guid God in s'providence
Sonnie restored to health and strength,
Nette ye could naither haud nor bind,
Barked sweet as songs o' Jenny Lind.

There's mony a ane wad like wee Nette,
But gowd's nae temptin tae me yet;
A' ither dugs ah'll sell for brass,
But na oor Cockie Nettie Lass.

J. Lunn Hood (1909)

Preface

WHILE writing this handbook, I have aimed to give a reasonably complete survey of the Dandie Dinmont Terrier. It must be said that I have not written as much on the breed as I could have wished, for this is one with a very full history indeed. I hope, however, that this revised contribution may perhaps prove helpful to those who keep Dandies and instructive, at least to some extent, to those who are not fully conversant with the breed's fascinating history.

It is usually the newcomers to a breed who buy books about it, and to these I would stress the great importance of character before fancy breed type and external characteristics. A true Dandie should be intelligent, of friendly, confident bearing and with a full quota of common sense. His physical structure is vitally important, of course, but true temperament comes first, especially in a dog such as this whose hard-living background and workmanlike qualities have moulded his character, his courage and adaptability to fulfil what he is today—a leading all-purpose dog who *is* a dog.

As regards workmanship, we can be sure that there are as good Dandie Dinmonts today as ever there were; and whenever the modern show Dandie is given an opportunity and adequate training to work he rarely fails to prove adept.

In public esteem he is held highly by those who know the breed and love it, but there are still many rungs in the ladder to be climbed towards general popularity, and although in my opinion there is still plenty of room in the land for the Dandie to introduce himself, it will be a sorry day for him and his admirers should he ever achieve the excessive popularity of the dogs who have suffered extensive commercialism and an undoubted ruination of correct type and temperament. However, progress in a breed is important, and there it must be or it will perish, for canine competition is strong. Conversely, too much conservatism is also wrong and breeders should make every effort to present this great and most desirable dog to the public notice, where once seen he would be universally appreciated.

I am indebted to the well-known breeders who have aided me with photographic material and vital statistics and information concerning the breed, particularly Mrs. Phyllis Salisbury, and to the Kennel Club for its usual great courtesy and help.

JOHN F. GORDON.

ROMFORD, *July, 1972.*

Contents

Thumbnail diagrams by Author

Anatomical diagrams by courtesy of Dr. M. Josephine Deubler of U.S.A.

I

Origin and History

THE fascination of any breed lies partly in its beginnings, and although most breeds can claim an interesting history the Dandie Dinmont Terrier has a particularly romantic place in the world of dogs for it is unique in the fact that it derived its name from a literary source. It owes this to Scotland's great novelist Sir Walter Scott, who named it thus in his immortal story *Guy Mannering*, published in 1814. This classic should be required reading for every Dandie enthusiast in order to assimilate 'atmosphere' of the breed's nominal beginnings and to assess for himself its true origin and usage in those days.

The actual origin of the Dandie is vague, and much disputative and contentious ink has been spilled over its history. Clearly it sprung from the several rough-coated Terrier breeds indigenous to the Scottish and English borderlands in the latter half of the eighteenth century, which in spite of some wide divergence in type were commonly known as 'Scotch' Terriers. That the Dandie emerged eventually as an individual type is accepted, but the event itself is lost in obscurity and cannot be dated, so many of the old Northern breeds being interrelated and not entirely dissimilar over a long period. Obviously, calculated crossings were made in those days to produce a short-legged, sturdy, bustling Terrier with a protective coat, peculiarly adapted for entering to, and killing ground vermin.

There is irrefutable evidence from the eighteenth century that the border gipsies, travelling tinkers and itinerant musicians used these dogs, not only for rough field work, poaching and help in the extermination of the otter and badger, but occasionally if not more frequently for badger-baiting, at which dubious sport considerable wagers would be laid on and against the dogs' prowess.

These little dogs were rough-coated, black, wheaten, red and colours between. They excelled at all the field sports and deep thicket work, being able to kill the sweetmart and foulmart, and some could kill a fox if they met up with one. Often enough though such a feat would prove beyond even the toughest and gamest of their kind, for the big Westmorland fox is a powerful, courageous beast, and rather a job for the Foxhound than for the lighter-going dog we now know as the Dandie Dinmont Terrier who, notwithstanding his short legs and long body, was a comparatively active dog and very game.

The Dandie's rough coat was ideally suited to meet prickly gorse coverts and the rough and rugged Liddesdale terrain, in parts inaccessible to Hounds and dogs much larger than our little low-slung bustler. The Dandie prototype was in those days much prized by the sportsmen of the area, as well as the gipsies and other nomads. They were the days when gameness and intelligence were considered paramount virtues; when a dog was needed for a tough job, and would do it with zest and efficiency, and never cry out if hurt. And from such stock comes the Dandie we know and breed today.

Some would have it, and J. H. Walsh ('Stonehenge') was one, that the Dandie comes from a rough-haired borderland Terrier crossed with a Dachshund. In his *Dogs of the British Isles* (4th edition, 1882), he expounds, stating that foreign stock was introduced to the native 'Scotch' Terrier by itinerant gipsies from the Continent. In this sentiment he had the support of D. J. Thomson Gray ('Whinstone'), author of *The Dogs of Scotland*, 1891, who claimed the Dandie Dinmont's eye was more typical of the Dachshund's than any indigenous Terrier breed, also that the ears of many specimens of his day resembled more those of the Dachshund than any other breed. Thus, both these experts preferred the theory of the Dachshund cross with a native Terrier, while others favoured the theory of the Dachshund crossed with the Otterhound or the Welsh Harrier, and these claimed for their argument the somewhat houndy carriage of the Dandie's stern and the shape and set-on of his ears. One has only to examine the picture of Carrick's Otterhound, 'Stanley' (see Plate), to concede some credence to such a theory. That such crosses as have been discussed were made and even furthered, is feasible, even probable, and the Hound–Terrier cross may well have been the source from which sprang the Bedlington Terrier, for it is almost certain that the produce of such a cross would be leggy.

However, the pure breed theory claimed the more adherents, and both Walsh and Gray departed largely from their contention, probably due to a public repudiation of the idea by Mr. E. Bradshaw Smith, referred to in later pages, and an acknowledged expert of his day. Charles Cook too, in his *The Dandie Dinmont Terrier*, 1885, stated that the breed 'is the product of long years of careful breeding or selection (the native rough Terrier being alone employed), the requirements of the Border country ultimately producing a Terrier adapted for its special work'. Cook avers that no other theory would account for the symptom of the silky 'top-knot' or mixed coat, both of them characteristic of the early 'Scotch' Terrier, of the borderlands, from which source the Dandie was undoubtedly evolved.

That the Bedlington Terrier and the Dandie Dinmont Terrier are first cousins and have temperamental and physical similarities there can be little doubt however, and the distinct 'top-knots' and pendulous filbert- or almond-shaped ears are common denominators in their Terrier make-up. Both breeds spring virtually from the same geographical area and trace to a similar history and origin.[1] In the late seventies it is on record that the Earl of Antrim achieved some notoriety and doubtless caused some cynical amusement by winning prizes in both the Dandie Dinmont Terrier and the Bedlington Terrier classes at a show with two dogs out of the same bitch by the same sire! Such an incident, if true, and there is no reason for disbelief, in itself would seem to indicate just how allied were the breeds at least in their early appearance.

However, to suppose that the breed has been kept absolutely free from crosses, whether occurring by accident or design, is to take up with the improbable. Doubtless in the past alien influence has affected the strain in parts, as indeed it has done with all breeds, although the influence may not now be apparent.

In the early days, it is on record that the Dandie was known as the 'Catcleugh' Terrier, 'Hindlee' Terrier or such, depending on the name of the farm where he was kept; or more generally by the

[1] Even Vero Shaw lumped the two breeds together when he gave them their first coloured illustration in his great *Illustrated Book of the Dog*, 1879–81.

generic names of 'Pepper and Mustard' Terrier, a local name in use long before Walter Scott's novel ever saw publication. This breed of dog was confined largely to the Coquet Water district of Northumberland, in the jealous ownership of gipsy tribes, Border tinkers, and 'muggers' who travelled much of the land abounding the Cheviots and Teviot. These to some extent popularised the breed, mainly due to their pride of ownership and boasting of the prowess of their dogs.

Prominent among the families who owned and bred these dogs were the Allans, Andersons, Anguses, Camells and Faas. All these and others besides cherished highly the little hard-bitten, rough-coated Terrier which could dispose so readily of the vermin of the countryside and afford them so much sport in their open-air lives.

The Allans of Holystone or 'Holestone', on the Coquet Water, near Rothbury, Northumberland, were said to have the purest strain of these Terriers and certainly it is known that the chief of this family, William Allan, better known as 'Piper' Allan, devoted himself so closely to the breed that at one time it became known locally as the 'Piper Allan Breed'. Willie Allan was born at Bellingham, Northumberland, in 1704, and is described as a bagpipe player, maker of spoons, baskets, brooms and a mender of pots and pans. A great fisherman, he kept a number of these game Terriers to indulge his fondness for otter-hunting. It is said that he had three special favourites among his dogs—Charley, Phoebe and Hitchem (Hitchem is sometimes wrongly recorded as Peachem). Allan's dogs were noted in the district and on many occasions were 'hired' by local landowners to dispose of marauding vermin on their property.

Much of Allan's history is recorded in Dr. John Brown's *Horae Subsecivae*, 1858–61. In a footnote it is recalled that on one occasion Lord Ravensworth employed Willie Allan and his dogs to clear the otters from his pond at Eslington Hall. This task was effected with such efficiency that his lordship coveted the dog Charley and instructed his steward to purchase him from Allan. The request at once offended the 'Piper' who exclaimed angrily 'By the *wuns*, his hale estate canna' buy Charley', a remark which promptly closed the discussion. On another occasion, the Duke of Northumberland (1749–66) offered Allan a farm rent free on his estate in exchange for Hitchem. The generous offer was immediately dismissed with the reply 'Na, na, ma Lord, keep yir ferum; what wad a piper do wi' a ferum?' Such refusals of tempting offers may not seem so surprising when one considers the type of man and the high opinion he had of his working dog. This is revealed in Allan's recorded observation on otter-hunting—'When my Peachem (Hitchem) gies mouth I durst always sell the otter's skin' which was his way of saying that as soon as 'Hitchem had marked the otter in its holt, he had as good as got it in his jaws and delivered it to his master!

'Piper' Allan died in February 1779, aged 75 years, and is buried in Rothbury churchyard. From him and other ordinary men of his kind came the breed we know now as the Dandie Dinmont Terrier. Little by little it found its way outside the nomadic circle of ownership into the homes of less itinerant folk—the country gentlemen, the yeomanry and local sportsmen, although still confined largely to the borderlands. Such families as the Davidsons of Swinnie, Robsons of Byrness, Telfords of Blindburn, Dodds of Catcleugh, Elliots of Cottonshope, Lilicoes of Jedwater, Donkins of Ingram, and the Bells of Hundalee Hill were but a few of the people who owned them.

The 'Piper' was succeeded by his sixth son James who was born of a gipsy mother at Hepple, Coquetdale, in 1734. An accomplish-ed bagpipe player, he assumed his father's appellation of 'Piper' and his flamboyant figure at Border race meetings and fairs, often in company of a Terrier or two did much again to bring the breed to the fore, even if only locally. He died in Durham in November 1810, aged 76 years. It is recorded that his son, a basket-maker, sold to Mr. Francis Somner of Yetholm a young dog named Old Pepper, purported to be a true lineal descendant of his grandfather's famous Hitchem. This dog was one of the grandparents of Mr. Somner's noted Shem referred to in later pages.

From the Allan family came much of the stock which was put on the market following upon the publication of Scott's *Guy Mannering* in 1814, at which point the breed achieved its fame and wider popularity in the country. Public demand at this stage was active, and many dogs and bitches were sold through such men as James Davidson, Francis Somner and Ned Dunn, who were in effect not only able to capitalise on the demand, but to obtain for themselves although unbeknowingly, a secure niche in the opening history of the breed. Others who helped to distribute stock in the early stages, especially to the south and south-west, were the Hon. G. H. Baillie of Mellerstain and Mr. G. Home of Carrolside.

That the general community believed that James Davidson 'discovered' the Dandie Dinmont Terrier must have been amusing to Davidson's contemporaries if not to the man himself, for all would have known that the breed had been in the hands of the Allans and other wandering tribes many years previously. *On the other hand, it may well be that Davidson by breeding principles peculiar to himself, and retaining only the shorter-legged and longer-backed specimens which he allowed to be called Dandie Dinmont Terriers, established with careful selection from the stock at his disposal, a more or less distinct type of his own.*

In *Guy Mannering*, these game wee dogs, although unfortunately not described by Walter Scott in the detail we would have wished, were ably woven into the fascinating Border tale, and the author's patent enthusiasm for them and for the steadfast character of their owners excited the imaginations of early nineteenth-century readers as indeed it does even today.

Scott himself, when Sheriff of Selkirkshire, got to know well these men of the Cheviots, and as he tells us in his notes to *Guy Mannering* the character of 'Dandie Dinmont' was drawn from no individual. A dozen at least of the stout Liddesdale farmers with whom he was acquainted and whose hospitality he had shared might well have laid claim to be the prototype of the rough but faithful, hospitable and generous man. It was not until 1816, or two years after *Guy Mannering* was published, that Sir Walter Scott saw James Davidson, to whom the name of 'Dandie Dinmont' had been given *by his acquaintances*. In Lockhart's *Life of Scott* is the following letter, written by Sir Walter in April 1816, which gives the proof:

> I have been at the Spring Circuit, which made me late receiving your letter, and there I was introduced to a man whom I never saw in my life before, namely, the proprietor of all the Pepper and Mustard family, in other words, the genuine Dandie Dinmont. Dandie himself is modest, and says, 'he b'lives it's only the dougs that is in the buik, and no' himself'.

Scott then goes on:

> Jamie Davidson, of Hyndlee, certainly looks Dandie Dinmont remarkably well. He is much flattered with the compliment, and goes uniformly by the name among his comrades, but has never read the book.

All this will show that when Scott wrote his book, Davidson was personally unknown to him, and it was only from Davidson's friends christening him Dandie Dinmont after the tale was written that attention was directed to him and his Terriers. It was not surprising, therefore, that Davidson having been dubbed in this name, his dogs should become known as Dandie Dinmont Terriers, instead of 'Peppers and Mustards'. Davidson being one of the largest owners of the breed in the borderlands would undoubtedly have cast a strong influence over its fortunes, and it was not long ere all these little dogs were known as Dandie Dinmonts. Idealists may still aver that the best of the breed comes from his original stock, and this may well be true, but it is clear that the farmer's stock was at that time entirely dependent upon what he could procure from the Allans in Holystone and similar sources of supply.

In history, whether political or canine, we must perforce commence at some given point, and as the legend of Davidson is outstanding as far as our breed is concerned, we have to begin with him. James Davidson was born on the farm of Wooplaw on the north side of Redwire in 1763. He became tenant of the hill farm of Hindlee (Hyndlee or Hindlea) on the Rule Water, owned by Lord Douglas where he remained until his death in Bongate, Jedburgh aged, 55 on 2nd January, 1820, leaving a widow and two sons. He was buried in his ancestral grave in Oxnam churchyard. In 1969 due to the fast disintegration of the tombstone a fund was raised to restore it, this being generously supported by Dandie owners on both sides of the Atlantic and the Abbotsford-Scott Fellowship. To Mr. George D. Shiell of Rennieston for his efforts in promoting this action the breed owes a deal of thanks.

Davidson was described as a man of 'strength, blunt honesty and hardihood'. He fitted admirably into the wild farm he rented on the very edge of the Teviotdale mountains in the parish of Southdean, Roxburghshire, having an abiding passion for the chase in all its forms, but especially in fox-hunting at which he was most adept. He had little time for packs of dogs, however, much preferring a more modest outing with a companion, perhaps two Hounds and a selected brace of Terriers of the kind we now call Dandie Dinmonts.

In 1869 *The Field* newspaper published a letter dated 2nd November of that year signed by J. Cumming Macdona. The Reverend J. C. Macdona was a Dandie owner and a judge of dogs, quite well-known in his day and his name carried some weight, so what he had to impart was generally accepted. Writing from the George Hotel, Melrose, deep in the heart of Dandie Dinmont country, he writes thus:

> Sir, In two months more it will be just half a century since brave old Dandie Dinmont breathed his last. Judging from Sir Walter Scott's description of his character, I cannot think he was the man to stick at a pound or two in the weight of his terriers one way or the other, provided they had been as he was wont to say, 'weel entered', and were of the same mettle as Young Pepper, 'that had lost a forefoot' or Mustard the Second 'that had been nearly throttled' in the famous otter hunt immortalised by Sir Walter Scott in *Guy Mannering*. I have however, in my researches into the history of this breed in this neighbourhood, near to its early home, this day been fortunate enough to meet with a document in Mr. James Davidson's own handwriting, to which his initial signature is attached. The perusal of this paper has convinced me as to the real origin of the Dandie Dinmont Terrier. The document bears all the marks of genuineness. The writing is yellow with years. The paper is the old-fashioned, hand-made letter paper—none of that cream-laid note, straw or satin, so much used nowadays. It was sent by Mr. Davidson to the late Hon. George H. Baillie of Mellerstain, and runs thus:
>
> 1800
>
> Tuggin, from A. Armstrong, reddish and wiry,
> Tarr, reddish and wire-haired; a bitch.
> Pepper, shaggy and light. Dr. Brown of Bonjedward.
> The race of Dandies are bred from the two last.
>
> J.D.

It appears that Dr. Brown of Bonjedward, gave Mr. Davidson, in the year 1800, Pepper and Tarr. This couple then, without doubt, are the first parents of all true-bred Dandie Dinmonts, being the original stock from whence all Mr. Davidson's generations of Mustards and Peppers sprang.

As Charles Cook in his monograph *The Dandie Dinmont Terrier*, 1885 points out, it is the date, i.e. '1800' and the word 'Dandies' which when associated with the date makes the reader doubt the authenticity of this document. Remember *Guy Mannering* was not published until 1814 and it was not until *that* year that the name 'Dandies' was known. Cook asks—'Is the date in the document the date on which it was written, or is it meant to show the date on which Mr. Davidson first got his terriers?' It seems that no one either then or now has been able to answer this question although it must have occurred, says Cook, to many who read the Rev. Macdona's letter.

It seems that Charles Cook, hot on the chase of the mysterious document at last managed to have sight of it, only to find that it varied substantially from the one revealed by Macdona. In the paper seen by Cook the date is given at '1890', which to him was a year some six or seven years in the future! Altogether the whole thing seems to have been a bit of a hoax and I am not surprised that Cook was never able to trace Dr. Brown of Bonjedward, although he did find out something about the 'A. Armstrong' referred to. He was believed a shepherd on the Wooplaw farm of James Davidson. Further, on checking the handwriting of James Davidson from authentic sources with the writing purported to be his on the document under discussion there were marked differences. The true hand of Davidson was that of a farmer, one unaccustomed perhaps to pen-holding, whereas the document showed the writing to be bold and distinct. Later it seems Cook had an expert examine the writing and it was pronounced as penned in 1818! The whole story, while fascinating indeed, is a mixed one and can have little bearing on who were in fact the Adam and Eve of Dandies. It is quite clear that a race of Peppers and Mustards abounded the area at the time when Mr. Davidson became first introduced to the breed. He certainly did not create the variety, but merely owned some and bred them to an extent that today he would be termed the owner of a large 'kennel'. No doubt others existed around the area who knew the breed more intimately than he, but by virtue of his possessions, his personality and the fact that he was dubbed 'Dandie Dinmont' by Scott in 1814 he became the main and leading character in the breed's history.

The following most interesting account of the Dandie's origin which appeared in *The Field* on 7th December, 1878, while savouring of the humorous may well contain much of the truth. At last it would seem to confirm that Davidson's original stock had its real source with the Border 'muggers' and gipsies . . . the letter reads as follows:

> Sir, I, as rather more than a sexagenarian and a Border man, and one who in almost his childhood took up with Dandies, can, I think, throw some light on the origin of the Dandies possessed by Mr. Davidson. The Border 'muggers' were great breeders of Terriers—the Andersons on the English side, and the Faas and Camells on the Scotch side. In their perambulations they generally met once or twice a year at Long Horsley, Rochester (the ancient Bremenium of the Romans), Alwinton, or some other Border village. If they could not get a badger, they got a foumart, wild cat, or hedgehog at which to try their dogs. The trials generally ended in a general dog-fight, which led to a battle-royal amongst the tribes represented. This afterwards led to a big drink and exchange of dogs. Jock Anderson, the head of the tribe, had a red bitch, who, for badger-drawing, cat, foumart, or hedgehog killing, beat all the dogs coming over the Border. Geordy Faa, of Yetholm, had a wire-haired dog Terrier, the terror of not only all other Terriers in the district, but good at badger, fox or foumart. They met at Alwinton, where Willy and Adam Bell (noted Terrier-breeders) had brought a badger they had got hold of at Weaford, near the Cheviots. Both the red bitch and other black Terrier drew the badger every time they were put in. 'Jock Anderson,' says Geordy, 'the dogs should be mated; let us have a grand drink, the man first doon to lose his dog.' 'Done,' says Jock. They sent for the whisky, which never paid the King's duty to Nevison's, at the little house, having agreed to pay 2*s*. a quart for it. Down they sat on the green, fair drinking; in eighteen hours Jock tumbled off the cart-shafts, and Geordy started off with the dogs. They were mated and

produced the first Peppers and Mustards, which were presented by Geordy to Mr. Davidson (Dandie Dinmont of *Guy Mannering*); strange to say the produce were equally the colour of pepper and mustard. The last pair I saw of what I consider perfect Dandies were Robert Donkin's at Ingram, near Alnwick, just before I left the North in 1838. I have been at shows, but could never identify any Dandies shown as at all like the original breed belonging to the Telfords of Blind Burn, the Elliots of Cottonshope, the Donkins of Ingram, and other Border farmers. I am not a doggy man, but like to see all old breeds kept distinct.

J. Davison.

Andover, Dec. 2. (1878).

However, we have no reason to doubt that Davidson by virtue of his calling as a farmer would have possessed a keen instinct and knowledge for breeding what was considered in those days to be the 'right stuff', and whatever brace of Terriers formed the foundation of his stock it is certain that subsequent stock would have been entirely on correct lines, primarily for character and gameness and then for desired type of a kind specially adapted for going to earth.

About the same time as Davidson took Hindlee, Mr. Stephenson of Plenderleigh farm procured a small Terrier from the source at Rothbury, noted for small ones. These dogs were also very dark and very rough-coated—dark rough coats were typical of any dog from Rothbury, and it is believed that Stephenson's Terriers were of the bluest blood.

A man close to Davidson in his connection with the breed was Ned Dunn of Whitelee, Carter Bar (at the top of Redesdale), who maintained a desirable strain, as did David and Arthur Kyle of Braidlee (Broad Lee). The former man was a noted wrestler, and was more active in the breed than his brother. Both were keen fox hunters and used the Dandie extensively at this sport.

A picture exists of Henry, 3rd Duke of Buccleuch, painted by Gainsborough in 1770, showing a Dandie varying hardly at all from the present-day type. At the 'Bowhill' kennels of Walter Francis, Duke of Buccleuch and Queensbury, K.G., and his brother Lord John Scott, many of the best specimens of the breed under the supervision of gamekeeper John Kerss, who succeeded Tom Fletcher in the post. These had been obtained in the main from Davidson's stock, as well as from Sir Walter Scott and 'Old' John Stoddart, the blacksmith at Selkirk. Stoddart, incidentally, was reputed to have the purest strain of Dandies on the Borders, between 1820 and 1830.

Stoddart owned the famous pair 'Dandie I' and Schan, the latter from Hindlee. The dog is described as very handsome, light grey-and-tan in colour, short in leg and broad behind, the gamest dog of his day. Schan, a little dark-grey bitch, was rather undershot, but dead game. Stoddart bred several litters from this pair, and from them came Dandie II, known as Dan, kept by the breeder for himself, and Charlie, a 12-lb dog good at fox and able to face anything. This one went to Mr. Thomas Tod of Drygrange.

The Duke of Buccleuch bought one of the bitches, eventually known as Bowhill Schan who was purported to have killed rats when she was only two months old [?] and others were sold to Lady Ravensworth, Mr. A. M'Culloch of Hot Baths, Leigh, Mr. J. S. Lyon of Kirkmichael and to Mrs. V. Douglas of Old Melrose and her brother Mr. R. Pringle of The Haining. All these fanciers bred in their turn, and did much to extend this desirable strain.

Sir Walter Scott of Abbotsford obtained his stock directly from James Davidson. Very little is known or recorded of Scott's dogs, apart from those he sold or gave to friends, although in the portrait of Sir Walter by Landseer a mustard Dandie is introduced and this is said to have been one of his dogs from Abbotsford. It seems rather shorter-bodied than present-day specimens, and has ears reminiscent of a Fox Terrier. Scott gave a brace of Dandies to Lord Polwarth of Mertoun. One of these, known as The Mertoun Dandie, was later used extensively at stud, and his name is prominent in many early pedigrees. Mr. J. S. Lyon of Kirkmichael had two from Sir Walter, and for many years rather amateurish illustrations of these dogs could be seen in the Kirkmichael house. There was also a picture to be seen there of the Lyon family painted by Gibson of Edinburgh, which although not particularly distinct in form, included a likeness of Spicy, who was by Scott's original Pepper in 1825 and Lyon's own Witchy. These, interbred with the Dandie obtained from John Stoddart's breeding, formed the nucleus of the Kirkmichael strain, which lasted only up to Lyon's death.

There is a picture of the first Lord Armstrong hanging in 'Cragside', the house he built many years ago in Rothbury, Northumberland. By his side can be seen a very representative Dandie Dinmont Terrier.

Another enthusiast was Thomas Stevenson of Jedburgh. He was considered an expert judge of the breed, and individuals from his kennel went to the Marquis of Tweeddale, who spent a great deal of money in acquiring the best specimens, and to Mr. Francis Somner of West Morriston. Mr. Somner was in fact one of the original serious breeders. His famous kennel of Dandies was founded in 1820 with the game 11-lb pepper bitch, Nettle, bred at Hindlee. First-class stock came out of Somner's kennels for the best part of thirty years. Davidson and he bred many Dandies between them to fill not only the demand for good stock created by Scott's novel, but for their own appreciation and gratification as lovers of the breed.

Of the many good ones bred by Somner, probably his most famous was a bluish-black grey named Shem, whelped in 1839, direct from Nettle. In 1842, Francis Somner moved to Kelso, and a number of specimens from his kennel went over to the ownership of Mr. Bradshaw Smith, old Shem among them. He kept a few, however, and in June 1844, he sold a useful brace of Terriers, including the brother of the noted May-Day to Count Robert de Portalis for Louis Philippe, King of France. The year 1852 saw the kennel dispersed and this was undoubtedly a loss to Dandies, for Francis Somner was a stickler for gameness in the breed. He never kept one unless it had been proven against fox or badger, neither would he breed from an untried dog. A pepper he bought from Yetholm was tried at a badger for four days, and finally drew Brock from his 9-ft box after taking severe punishment. At this point, perhaps, it is worthy of comment that such anecdotes seldom record whether the badger under trial had taken water and nourishment during capture, an extremely unlikely event; consequently it is not such a great achievement to draw badger in such circumstances as might at first be thought. However, there is no doubt that Dandies of the period under review were good game creatures and most of them would have tried their skill at the task.

Dr. William Brown and his brother John ('Rab') of Melrose were both very keen on the breed, and the latter in his *Horæ Subsecivæ*, 1858–61, introduced the Dandie in a chapter entitled 'Our Dogs'. They owned Crab, John Pym and his son Puck. James Scott of Newstead, a boyhood friend of Davidson, was in essence a purist so far as his beloved breed was concerned. He died in 1874, but contributed much valuable material to the history of the Dandie Dinmont. He was almost certainly the main participator under the pseudonym 'Border Sportsman', in a series of acrimonious letters which appeared in *The Field* newspaper in 1869 concerning the history of the breed.

Mr. Nicol Milne of Faldonside obtained his first Dandie from his brother-in-law Mr. C. Wilson of Otterburn, owner of the game mustard dog, Old Jock, previously owned by James Davidson. He had also a yellow bitch named Jenny out of a black-and-tan bitch from the widow of Ned Dunn, the Whitelee gamekeeper whose preference was for the lighter weight Dandies, so it is said. Jenny was famous in her day, had several litters and threw some excellent stock. In the Blackwoodhouse records, kept so faithfully by Mr. E. Bradshaw Smith, she is described in a note made in June 1843 as a very good specimen of the breed. Milne kept a good kennel, but unfortunately no records were maintained.

Mr. James Aitken of Maryfield House, Edinburgh, had his first one about 1840. In 1846 he acquired the bitch, Meadow, mentioned by 'Stonehenge', bred in 1844 at Birseslees, Long Newton, Roxburghshire, by Sir George H. Douglas, Bt., of Springwood Park who was very active in the breed with his gamekeeper William Broadworth, a keen enthusiast. Meadow was by Douglas's Pepper out of Schan who was by 'Old' John Stoddart's Dandie I out of Schan of Hindlee. Pepper himself was bred by Mr. P. S. Lang of Selkirk.

Some confusion exists in records between Meadow and May-Day owned by Mr. D. M'Dougall of Cessford, born about 1836 and later sold to Mr. E. Bradshaw Smith. This is perhaps understandable when one considers the phonetic resemblance of these two names when uttered in the Scottish dialect.

Around 1846 Aitken bought a young dog, Shem, from Dr. William Brown of Melrose by John Brown's John Pym (a son of

Mr. Somner's Shem) out of one of Mr. Nicol Milne's bitches. The ensuing progeny was later crossed by Mr. Aitken with stock from the Telfords of Blindburn and other good strains. Dr. H. Grant of Hawick was another outstanding sportsman of the period. He maintained a small pack of Dandie Dinmonts, and was a regular hunter of the Teviot otter.

H. H. Dixon ('The Druid') in *Field and Fern; or Scottish Herds and Flocks* (*South*), 1865, wrote that to pass through Hawick without an introduction to Dr. Grant and his Dandies was not to be thought of. Grant owned Nettle and Pepper obtained from Paul Scott of Jedburgh, and Shamrock from Sir George Douglas's gamekeeper. *This* Shamrock from the Birseslees branch of Dandies was bred by James Scott of Newstead from the bitch Vixen by Pepper (or Brown Pepper or Pepper II). Dr. Grant was a believer in the supremacy of Davidson's stock, and was almost fanatical in his adulation of the breed and its capabilities. He is even said to have quoted at times from the Greek poet Oppianus to prove that the 'crook-limbed and black-eyed' breed were natives of Britain at the time of the Roman invasion.

Mr. E. Bradshaw Smith was one of the early notables in the breed. A native of Dumfriesshire, his home was at Blackwood-house, Ecclefechan, but he lived in Roxburghshire about 1840. He started his kennel in 1841 with the best from Francis Somner's stock, also with purchases from D. M'Dougall of Cessford and Hugh Purves (or Purvis) of Leaderfoot, who it is reported did at times use a brindle Bull Terrier to his bitches to increase their progeny's gameness and stamina! Other stock Smith acquired from Messrs. Frain of Trows, Stoddart of Selkirk, Milne of Faldonside, Kerss the 'Bowhill' gamekeeper, R. Pringle of The Haining and many others. He did in fact buy whenever he saw a good one, and the variety of strains with which he commenced and maintained his kennel enabled him to dispense for many years with outside bloodlines, many of which failed on their own account within a short period because of excessive inbreeding.

Mr. E. Bradshaw Smith's kennels kept going until his death in 1882, and only then there showed some deterioration in his stock. It is believed by some that the Dandie Dinmont Terrier, by virtue of unscrupulous dealing in non-typical and unsound stock which prevailed in this period, may well have fallen by the wayside, had it not been for Mr. Smith's enthusiastic efforts on behalf of the breed. Some say even that he saved the breed from extinction in a very black period of its history. One of his best dogs was Dirk Hatterick, written of as the 'Incomparable' Dirk. Only occasionally did Smith introduce new stock, and between 1854 and 1876 he bought from Mr. J. B. Richardson of Dumfries Jack and Jenny both by Smith's own dog, Pepper (the sire of Dirk) out of Mr. Richardson's Myrtle in 1868. He also bought the mustard dogs, Otter and Badger, these by Smith's Marmot out of Richardson's Topsy, whelped in 1876. Further new stock came in with Gyp (by Dr. Grant's Teddy out of Dr. R. Riddell's Mary I) from Mr. William Poole. Two puppies came from the Rev. S. Tenison Mosse, who owned the dog, Shamrock. These two were Jock, by Dirk out of Lyon's bitch, and Brock, by the same sire out of Rev. J. C. Macdona's Meg, bred by Nicol Milne. In 1854 he bought from Milne the last of Jenny's progeny in Dandie (B).

The Blackwoodhouse strain was in direct line from the original 'Peppers and Mustards' of Hindlee. Mr. Smith presented one of his famous Dandies to Queen Victoria at Windsor, who had already had one Dandie given her in 1842 by Prince Albert. Blackwoodhouse dogs were entered regularly to badger and fox, and gameness was preserved and cherished. In 1880 he had two dogs and three bitches deliberately poisoned in their kennels by an unknown hand, and two years later Smith himself died in Geneva, where many years previously he had buried his old Shem. The dogs were dispersed throughout the border counties after his death, although the mustard dog, Birkie, was retained as a companion by his widow. 'Eaglesfield' Bradshaw Smith kept his records in detail in the form of a day-by-day report, and the facts recorded are considered complete and are never subject to doubt. His efforts on behalf of the Dandie and the vital history he recorded for the benefit of those that followed in the breed render his name high on the list of those who have served and campaigned the Dandie Dinmont.

An enthusiast who did much for Dandies in their initial stage was Mr. Matthew Charlton of the noted Charlton family of Brundonlaws at the head of Oxnam Water. He was connected with the Davidson family, and later was to be in attendance at the first meeting of the Dandie Dinmont Terrier Club. A lifetime friend of Mr. Nicol Milne of Faldonside he was adamant on the gameness of the Dandie, and although he bred the well-known Border Minstrel most of his dogs were more at home dealing with fox and badger. (Capt. I. Morlais Thomas has something to say of the foulmart in his *Welsh Terrier Handbook*, 1959. He quotes several allusions to the animal in early Welsh poems and it seems to have featured in early Breton and Gaelic ballads too—Author.)

2

Early Dog Shows and Exhibitors

DOG shows came well into general favour in the latter half of the last century, and classes were provided for Dandie Dinmont Terriers at such early dates as 1861 in Manchester and 1862 in Birmingham. In 1863, Mr. James Aitken of Edinburgh sent a dog to the Cremorne show, and got with it only a third prize, the higher awards being withheld. At an eventful show at Birmingham in 1867, the two judges withheld all the prizes and the Rev. W. J. Mellor, who had his Bandy entered on that occasion, is reported as being far from pleased at the decision.

In fact, some of the dogs entered in the early days were clearly of doubtful authenticity as far as their pedigrees were concerned, there being a great diversity of type exhibited at certain shows. In the 1867 show just referred to, Mr. Matthias Smith, the judge who withheld the prizes started a press war with all the breed people against him when he stated openly that all the entries were no more than mongrels! On 16th November, 1867, *The Field* published a letter from Smith which read:

The Dandie Dinmont

Sir, I must ask you kindly to allow me space in your next issue for a few remarks, which cannot, I take it, fail to be of interest to those of your readers who have an interest in, and care for, the dog called the Dandie Dinmont. It is because of late there has been much division of opinion as to what is, or what is not, the true and genuine breed of this particular dog, that I the more readily venture to state my own opinion on the matter. It will be in the recollection of most dog-fanciers that for two years in succession I had the pleasure of being one of the judges at the Birmingham Show, and also that I did, with my brother judges, disqualify and refuse to award prizes to certain dogs entered as Dandies. It is not now my intention to put myself on the defence because the course I took as a judge did not meet with the entire approval of sundry exhibitors and others, nor is my intention to attempt to reply to the one-sided and palpably false argumentative reasoning which has since appeared in public correspondence on the subject; but my sole object in addressing you is to give your readers the benefit of my experience and opinion at the same time adducing statements of fact which no dispassionate dog-fancier can possibly gainsay or deny. I would beg then that members of the Dandie Club, and Dandie fanciers generally, would either admit that my opinion is entirely the correct one, or, if not correct, show in a truthful and logical way that it is an erroneous one. The position, then, which I take is this: That the so-called Dandies which are constantly receiving prizes at our leading dog shows are not of the pure Dandie Dinmont breed, but are mongrels. I admit that I have devoted much time, thought, and money to make myself familiar with the numerous varieties called Dandies, and I generally allow that those judges whose knowledge of the Dandie is not so matured as my own ought not altogether be blamed; but if they persist in hugging ignorance, and pandering to that which ought to give way to an exact and true knowledge of the matter which is really within their reach, then indeed blame is their deserved portion. It is pitiable to note that from time to time prizes have been awarded to dogs which differed from each other on points which admit of no difference whatever in the case of dogs of a pure and special breed; and I am prepared to say that from time to time standards of excellence for these 'hybrid' Dandies have been made so as to suit the particular animal owned by the fanciers; and this, too, with the idea of carrying out to a greater degree the determination of some that this so-called Dandie shall be regarded as the true breed of Dandie. Further, I would say that certain gentlemen, in order to establish a breed peculiar to their own fanciful imaginations, have invented from time to time pedigrees worked out, as it would appear, from certain celebrated kennels; indeed, so far has this gone, that many now come to regard these prize hybrids as belonging to the true and original breed of Dandies as mentioned by Sir Walter Scott in his *Guy Mannering*. Never was there a greater error, and I take it that the time has come when we should try once more to raise up amongst us the true breed of the Dandie Dinmont, and repudiate as unquestionable mongrels the bandy-legged, out-elbowed dogs which too often, alas! take off the prizes which should properly go to the genuine breed. Who does not remember the description given by Sir Walter Scott of old Davidson's dogs, which he prided himself so much on, especially the terriers Peppers and Mustards; and then, further on in the story, how it is stated that 'The Deuke himself has sent as far as Charlie's Hope to get ane o' Dandy Dinmont's Pepper and Mustard terriers'? Now, it would seem to me that those dogs were not what the hybrid Dandies of the present day are; for, as he says—'I had them a' regularly entered, first wi' rottens (rats), then wi' stots (weasels), and then wi' the tods (foxes) and brocks (badgers); and now they fear nothing that ever cam' wi' a hairy skin on't.' When in Scotland a few weeks since, I made a point of going to Abbotsford, where, as your readers are aware, is a portrait of a Dandie Dinmont painted by the late Sir Edwin Landseer, which dog, when alive, belonged to the late Sir Walter Scott. I affirm that this dog was never the same dog as the mongrel Dandie prize-dog of today. Some of your readers may also be aware that Mr. E. Bradshaw Smith, of Blackwood House, Ecclefechan—'the best authority, perhaps, in the world', had a pure Dandie Dinmont Terrier from old Davidson, and, when this dog died, had it stuffed. I have seen this dog, and I say of this, as in the case of Sir Walter's dog painted by Sir Edwin Landseer, that it is totally different from the so-called Dandie of today.

It is further stated that this gentleman has in his kennels a great many dogs descended in direct line from the Charlie's Hope kennels of Peppers and Mustards. These dogs I have seen and carefully examined, and my opinion respecting them is similar to that above expressed concerning Landseer's painting of Scott's Dandie and Mr. Bradshaw Smith's 'stuffed' one. Further, in support of my argument, I may say that I have seen a Dandie stuffed called Old Pepper, which belonged to Mr. Pat Lang, banker at Selkirk. Dogs owned by Mr. Locke of Selkirk, by Mr. Scott of Jedburgh; by Mr. Miller—'a prize taker' of Moffat; numbers owned of different strains, by small and limited fanciers—all without one exception differ entirely from the portrait at Abbotsford and the 'stuffed' one at Blackwood House. Further in support of my argument, some of the oldest breeders of the so-called Dandies admit they are mongrels, and not 'pure', because it is quite a chance if in a litter of their pups one will find two alike.

Matthias Smith.

125 Hyde Park Road, Leeds.

Of course, these were the days, early days in the breed when it was in the 'melting pot' as far as exhibition work was concerned. The men who worked these dogs while trying to maintain type and strain, were never averse to running dogs of doubtful yet possibly similar type with their purebreds if the former sort worked well. The same applied to those interested in dog shows—many knew very little as to what was wanted in a Dandie and kept and exhibited specimens which often ran far short of the ideal. Later when a proper knowledge as to what constituted a good Dandie was disseminated, the true breed picture became sharper and fixed in the eyes of reputable breeders. The poor sorts were culled and only Dandies with reliable antecedents were used in breeding programmes.

Improvement in Dandie type and quality progressed although for a few more years certain incidents evoking argument and acrimony in the show ring were recorded.

Then the writer Mr. Rawdon B. Lee's Sir Douglas, whose pedigree was doubted by Lee's rivals, won a great deal, including a first prize at the Border Show in Carlisle in 1871. This dog was around 27 lb in weight, and his prize caused much dissent in Dandie circles of the day. Second to him at the show was Punch owned by Mr. G. Coulthard, by the same sire, Harry.

At the same show Mr. E. Bradshaw Smith had four entries, but these were passed over as being in poor condition, among them the dog known as the 'Incomparable' Dirk, and as I have already pointed out it was reported towards the close of Mr. Smith's career with Dandies that a certain decadence had set in his stock owing to continual inbreeding.

Round about the same period Robert and Paul Scott, both pedlars in the Jedburgh district, were becoming noted for their excellent Dandie stock, and they developed their strain for gameness and show points. Peachem, a noted dog they owned was taken to shows on various occasions, and at Crystal Palace Show in 1872 he was first in the class provided for Dandies. Robert Scott's pithy remark concerning his assessment of Peachem's worth is amusing—'Eh, eh! It's ainlie the joodges can beat Peachem!' The dog was described as a good specimen 'not too big, not too little, good in coat, colour and top-knot, nicely domed in skull, shapely, well arched in body and not too crooked in front'.

The first Dandie Dinmont Terrier Club show, a notable event was held on the 4th January, 1877, in Carlisle, with Mr. William Poole and Mr. J. B. Richardson judging, the awards being made by points. An entry of eighty-five Dandies competed, and the system of points judging adopted would seem to have achieved very little for the winners were of vastly different types. Shamrock, a 20-lb dog owned by the Rev. S. Tenison Mosse, was awarded 78 points out of the possible 100, and Mr. W. Carrick's mustard dog, Harry Bertram, a dog of 27½ lb received 59 points. There is no further record of Dandies having been judged by this method, so doubtless the winners were not so popular on the day! These were the years when the Dandie Dinmont achieved the height of his popularity. Big shows scheduled classes for the breed, and leading exhibitors campaigned the breed wherever they saw an opportunity.

Some of those working in the breed's interests were giants of the dog world such as the Rev. S. Tenison Mosse, Capt. H. Ashton, Messrs. J. H. Murchison, James Locke of Selkirk, W. Carrick of Carlisle, James Cook of Edinburgh, A. Irving and W. Poole of Dumfries, A. H. T. Newcomen of Kirkleatham, W. Dorchester of Reading, M. Slater and G. Coulthard of Carlisle, and J. Finchett of Llanrwst, Wales, one of the biggest breeders eighty years ago. Following them, or almost contemporary with them, were Capt. I. Keene, Dr. G. Haddon of Melrose, the Rev. S. Tiddeman, Mrs. M. E. Grieve of Redhill, Mrs. R. Peel Hewitt of Kensington, and Messrs. R. Stordy, D. J. T. Gray, A. Weaver, A. Kemball Cook, W. Walker, J. Sherwood Jnr., J. Clarke of

London, J. Nutsford of Carlisle, E. W. H. Blagg, J. Flinn of Portobello, G. Shiel of Hawick, C. Cornforth of Leiston, J. E. Dennis of Gateacre, Alex. Downie of Eaglesfield, J. Houliston and James Morley of Dumfries, and Thomas Maxwell, who struggled hard in his lifetime to ensure the Dandie did not degenerate.

These were followed by a further number of enthusiasts, among them Archie Steel of Kelso, Mrs. Kate Spencer of Ewell, Mrs. Lloyd Rayner of Ormskirk, Miss M. Collyer of Fulham, and Mrs. J. Tweddle of Liskeard, W. G. Copeland of Kirk Langley, H. J. Bidwell of Frimley, J. W. Oram of Carlisle, while for a short time the Earl of Antrim was an admirer of the breed . . . indeed it is he who is referred to in the opening chapter of this book as having won prizes in both the Dandie Dinmont and Bedlington Terrier classes with two dogs out of the same bitch by the same sire!

Classes for the breed appeared at many shows as popularity progressed, and at Manchester in 1894 Mr. J. Brough's Bella Coota made her successful debut and at the same venue in 1896 Mr. Alexander Downie's Blacket House (formerly Piper Allan) won a first prize.

In the latter part of the last century Mr. William Mason ('Hayrigg') started breeding Dandies in his home town of Ecclefechan. He had four to commence with, their sire being owned by Ned Scott, a travelling Border tinker. He later bred in partnership with a relative, Mr. A. Lockhart of Eaglesfield, but on Lockhart's death continued alone. He bred right up to the First World War and kept one bitch, Nettle, later registered as Hayrigg Honey. She is behind many present-day Dandies and she and her daughter, Saida (Hayrigg Heyday), produced good stock to Ch. Ellwyn Kith, some of whom were exported to America by Provost Dalgleish. Mr. Mason maintained a strong female line for many years and through Jack Mason it has become an important family. Hayrigg Honey goes back tail female to Daisy, Topsy, Byker Peggey, Buttercup (dam of Jack Mason), Kirtle Trim, Border Beauty, Nell II, Tuss (or Fuss), Fairy (Lockhart's) and Wasp (3403). This Wasp is rather difficult to identify as there are over a score of registered and unregistered Wasps to be found in records. Mr. Mason was far more interested in entering his stock to prove gameness rather than to exhibit. His death some years ago was a sad loss to Dandie people. His son, Mr. Carl Mason, reports that one of the few bitches his father bought was Musk, a litter sister to Ch. Salismore Mustard and thoroughly game and fearless at otter.

Mr. Andrew MacCulloch was a keen devotee of the breed, and strived always to maintain a particular type which he considered correct. All his Terriers were true Dandies in character. They had the typical weasel-shaped body, were usually good in head expression, and of medium size for 'Andra' (as he was affectionately known) disliked the heavy kinds. His dogs usually had well-splayed front feet, for their owner contended that so equipped they could better throw aside the soil when digging in. This caused some argument between him and Mr. T. Rutherford, referred to later, who believed the true Dandie should own straight strong feet as it is a dog intended primarily to bolt its quarry rather than dig for it. Andrew MacCulloch had his first Dandie in the early seventies, his first pedigree one being Giffnock Tinker (Mac Siccar out of Princess Flora). He later owned Ch. Giffnock Ferret (1254A) born in 1894 and the 'Giffnock' Dandies —Sol, Pedlar, Twilight, Smuggler and Whim.

A sporting incident recalled by Mr. MacCulloch concerns the sire of his first Dandie who was wagered on by his owner to kill 50 rats in 15 minutes, the dog losing if any one of the rats he grabbed moved the length of itself after being dropped. However, the dog in question observed the rules closely, and disposed of the rats with over a minute to spare! Mr. MacCulloch was contemporary with Mr. John Millican of Scotby ('Honest John' of the 'Scotby' prefix) with whom he was good friends. Millican bred Ch. Scotby Tip Top, Scotby Daisy and Scotby Badger—in fact both men bred some great dogs during their association with the breed.

Mr. William Poole, a Dumfries chemist, owned Charlie, an important stud dog, and Young Charlie. He exhibited Vic (3098) born in 1871 and later sold him to Mr. G. Coulthard of Carlisle. Mr. Poole kept all his pedigrees with great care and present-day fanciers owe him a debt on this score at least. Mrs. M. E. Grieve of Redhill owned and showed many good ones, including Ch. Thistle Dandie a mustard dog who won five C.Cs., Ch. Milverton Yet, Bonnie Jeanne and Black Lug, and her favourite, Thistle Grove Gallant, who travelled everywhere with her.

About 1892 Mrs. R. Peel Hewitt of Walton-on-the Hill, Surrey, a prominent member of the Ladies' Kennel Association, owned and bred many fine specimens including the pepper, Ch. Tommy Atkins (34905), an 'Ettrick' dog. She also bred the mustards, Ch. Gordon Daisy, Ch. Gordon Prince and Gordon Beauty and the pepper, Ch. Tartan Chief. Mr. M. P. Lucas ('Milverton') of Leamington and Kelso was another active breeder owning the celebrated Border Rover in the seventies, and the Chs. Milverton Lady, Milverton King and Milverton Duke. Mr. J. Locke of Selkirk took much care in his choice of stock, selecting only those he considered were the possessors of authentic pedigree. He had Sporran (3903), Gyp (3057) born in 1872 with a pedigree back to Davidson of Hindlee, Doctor (5556) born 1875, Tarr (5574) born 1874, Riddell (6644) born 1876, Vixen (6661) born 1874, Whiskey (7678), Ginger II (9570) born 1879 and Selkirk Gyp (10897) born 1878.

Mr. John Wilson of the 'Glassford' prefix was known as the 'Father of the Dandie Fancy'. He was a barber in Ardrossan and Glasgow, the Glassford Street shop being a popular rendezvous for the doggy men of his day. A contemporary with such figureheads of the breed as Paul Scott, Archie Steel, Andrew MacCulloch, Johnny Honliston, to mention only a few, he bought his first Dandie from Bob Kerr of Balgar in 1879. Later, he bought a brace from J. Harding of Dumfries, these by the noted Dirk. One of these was a saddleback named Wambo. You seldom if ever see them today, the tan markings coming up over the hips giving the pepper coat an impression of being mounted with a mustard saddle. The marking, taboo today, was only a slight handicap to a dog then, unlike the chocolate-coloured coat which was detested. John Wilson bred some famous ones—Glassford Kathie, later sold to Mrs. T. Simpson Shaw of 'Alpin' note went for £30. She exported the bitch to America, the new owner Mrs. McLay having a deal of success with her. Kelvin Queen and Kelvin Jock were another great brace and Campsie Jock also helped to make John Wilson's name. He judged first at an Ingram, Burbank show in 1883 when Ch. Border King won in dogs. He was also known as a judge of Clydesdale and Scottish Terriers. He was the father of Dr. John A. Wilson of Pleasley, the present owner of 'Glassford' kennels and a clever breeder.

He has produced many fine winners including Ch. Glassford Clementina, Glassford Ruby, Glassford Quicksilver and Chs. Glassford Diadem, Glassford Curate and others, the last-named being the only Champion descended tail-male from Dirk, 'the Incomparable'.

Dr. Wilson's latest, Ch. Glassford Craigvar Cover Girl and Ch. Glassford Whin, the latter a veteran now, are really fine specimens and do justice to the name of this noted and long-established kennel.

Mr. David MacCulloch, the eldest son of Andrew MacCulloch ('Giffnock'), was a member of the Scottish Kennel Club committee, and for some time secretary of the Dandie Dinmont Terrier Club, being their show manager for many years. He occasionally judged, but did very little breeding or showing. He died in 1946. Mr. Andrew D. Lawson of Caddon, Galashiels, was born in 1882. A great worker for the breed, he succeeded D. MacCulloch as secretary of the Club, and was a noted figure in amateur athletics. He owned Caddon Lass and several other useful exhibits and bred and showed Dandies all his life under the 'Caddon' prefix. He died also in 1946.

Mr. W. A. F. B. Coupland of Dumfries bred and owned several good ones. He had the celebrated Ch. Border King[1] (16044), a 23-lb pepper dog by Badger (6636) out of Queen of the Borders (16938). He also bred the pepper, Border Prince (13815) by Richardson's Shem out of the same bitch. In addition he was for some time chairman of the South of Scotland Dandie Dinmont Terrier Club, and was on that club's list of judges.

Mr. W. Dorchester of Reading owned some prominent Dandies, among them Cloudie born 1872 by Kilt out of Missie, and Jock

[1] Ch. Border King enjoyed a long and successful career. He was bred by Mr. Coupland and sold at an early age to Mr. J. Flinn of Portobello, under whom he won his first prizes. He was then sold to Mr. D. Baillie of Lochmahen and took further awards under his handling. Eventually he was spotted by Mr. G. A. B. Leatham of Tadcaster, the 'Ainsty' wizard, and brought up by him. Leatham bought skilfully and widely (mainly from Mr. A. Weaver, the 'Lemster' breeder) and piloted the best of his acquisitions to fame in short time. Border King was exhibited widely by Leatham and soon reached Championship status, and was regarded by many authorities as of the finest type of Dandie of the eighties and early nineties. In fact illustrations of this dog were used to represent the Dandie Dinmont in books and journals not only in Britain but in the U.S.A., Holland and Sweden . . . one of the best-known drawings of him was one by R. H. Moore—Author.

who was bred by Mr. C. Cook and whose pedigree features in Vol. I of the *Kennel Club Stud Book*. He also had Toper (3095) born in 1868 by Nicol Milne's Old Jock out of Schann, sister to Shamrock (3089).

Among the earlier show-goers was Mr. George T. Hempson ('Astral') who strongly favoured the Dandie in spite of his interest in other breeds. He bred them from the early eighties having purchased from Mr. C. H. Lane (owner of Ch. Laird and then secretary of the Dandie Dinmont Terrier Club) the good bitch, Leah II, who thus became the foundation bitch of the Hempson kennels and who won regularly. Among other Dandies he owned was Astral Craig and Astral Rip.

Mrs. Lloyd Rayner's kennels were situated in the beautiful valley of Kentmere (which gave its name to her prefix)1000 ft. above sea level in the wilds of Westmorland Fells. She owned many good ones, but the founder of her kennel, Ch. Blacket House Yet 1249, was a mustard, whelped March 1893. He was used by Birkie III out of Meg Merrilees and bred by Mr. A. Downie who sold him to Mrs. Lloyd Rayner for £70. He sired many fine winners including notably the great Graythwaite Dhu out of March Judy. Mrs. Rayner owned also the lovely Ch. Ancrum Fanny 361, a pepper whelped in 1894 by Ancrum Pearl II out of Robertson's Gyp. The late Irwin Scott considered Fanny the best bitch he had ever seen and almost perfect. Others in the 'Kentmere' kennel included Graythwaite Jock, Fairfield Waif, the dam of many winners. Also inmates were March House Blackie, Kentmere Lily and Graythwaite Dirk. Mrs. Lloyd Rayner kept a small pack of Pocket Beagles, hounds which were quick away after the Fell fox with her Dandies in full cry and with whom the lady had many enjoyable hunts.

Mr. G. A. B. Leatham of Thorp Arch, Tadcaster (later of Boston Spa), used the prefix 'Ainsty'. He had one of the largest kennels owned by any one man in the late eighties. He was in fact known as 'The Dandie King', and was a member of the Kennel Club and both specialist clubs. He seldom had less than ten couples at any one time, not including the puppies, and was winner of the team prize on many occasions. Thorp Arch Terriers were always well trained for going to earth and Leatham claimed they were the gamest on land or in water. He began showing in

1887, and judged at Cruft's in 1890. He presented Ainsty Gem to H.R.H. The Duke of Clarence.

Among his well-known ones were, of course, the famous Ch. Border King (16044) and Ettrick (21328), Ch. Heather Sandy (23295), Ch. Ainsty Dandie (32319), Ch. Heather Peggy (23326), Ch. Darkie Deans (23287), Little Pepper II (25579), Ainsty Belle (25595), Davie Deans (25571), Ainsty Jock (32332), Ainsty Topper (34866), Ainsty Marvel (39374), Ainsty Duchess (25618), Victoria Regina (23348), Doctor Deans (25572) and Netherby II (27740). He also owned the game Ainsty King (27723), a noted show winner of 19 lb, breeder, date of birth and pedigree unknown, and who was reported to have stood for 1½ hours at a badger.

John B. (J. B.) Richardson registered his prefix of 'Slitrig' in 1920 from his home in Hawick. He should not be confused with the other J. B. Richardson of Dumfries, a name equally familiar to Dandie enthusiasts, but who died earlier. From the 'Slitrig' kennels came the great-headed mustard dogs, Ch. Brawny Kim, Ch. Glenfarg Chief and Highland Chief, and the home-bred Dandies, Slitrig, Masher, Rob Roy and Hawick Masher. Among the bitches were the home-bred Nancy Pretty, Cinderella, Slitrig Colleen, Slitrig Dolly, Slitrig Molly, and Burpham Andra, a mustard bred by Mrs. D. M. W. Wolseley in 1926.

Mrs. T. M. Simpson Shaw was one of the breed's staunchest supporters and enthusiasts for over fifty years, and her 'Alpin' prefix led the field for many decades. She began breeding Dandies seriously in 1893, showing first at Chelmsford in 1896 under the Rev. Mr. Tiddeman. Her first bitch of note was Diana Vernon, given to her by Mr. Frederick Drumflower of Wigtownshire. She first used Mrs. R. Peel Hewitt's Ch. Tartan Chief and later Ch. Puff owned by T. B. Potterton ('Boughton'), and bred her first puppies of note in 1897. Her Ch. Alpin Viceroy was by Lucas's Ch. Milverton King ex Alpin Golightly. She then bought the pepper dog Cargen Pilot from T. S. and R. Thomson ('Cairnside') of Dumfries, Pilot being the litter brother of Ch. Cargen Duke. She also purchased Giffnock Nettle and from George Shiel ('Thistle Grove') of Hawick she bought two Dandies who later became Ch. Alpin Stormer and Ch. Alpin Slitrig. The former, who was inbred to Ch. Thistle Grove Dargai and Thistle Grove Ben, was responsible for fixing the great type and quality of the 'Alpin' stock. Later Mrs. Simpson Shaw bred the 21-lb Ch. Alpin Raider in 1920. He sired at least fourteen Champions, including Ch. Darenth So Wise and Ch. Alpin Oberon, who in turn was himself the sire of Chs. Alpin Oracle, Alpin Osiris and several others. The Chs. Alpin Lochinvar and Alpin Roro were also bred by her. Mrs. Simpson Shaw was secretary of the Dandie Dinmont Terrier Club in 1902, and created much interest for the breed in a breed bulletin she edited called *The Supplement*.

Mr. and Mrs. G. Foster Rawlins ('Potford') maintained a large kennel between the wars, and won extensively at the premier shows. They bred two famous dogs in one litter. These were the Chs. Potford Plunderer and Potford Highlander by Ch. Friern Dandie out of the lovely mustard bitch, Nellie Tempest. Mr. Foster Rawlins was particularly noted for his presentation of the 'Potford' dogs.

Mr. John Skilling was one of the old fanciers who saw much of the work done in the first two decades of this century. Born in 1845 he died in 1922 and had known Mr. E. Bradshaw Smith and the Blackwoodhouse kennels at Eaglesfield. He loved small Dandies, and was the owner-breeder of Skilling's Piper, a dog who is responsible tail-male for many present-day winners, and made the 'O.G.' ('Old Ginger') Line famous.

Another great lover of the breed was Mr. T. Rutherford. He owned among others the pepper Thistle Grove Pat and Ch. Otter Witch and later Ch. Salismore Sovereign, a beautiful mustard dog bred by Mrs. D. Lane of Wokingham by Ch. Darenth Badger out of Shetland Princess. Miss. J. Horsfall ('Hillary') bred among others the noted Ch. Hillary Timothy who was owned and shown by the late Mrs. Leycester Penrhyne ('Clane') who also bred, owned and exhibited a fine mustard in Ch. Sandy of Clane. The 'Clane' affix is still carried on with great success in the breeding field and show ring by her daughter, Mrs. V. Sage of Ilminster.

The Hon. Mrs. Susan McDonnell ('Darenth') kept a very large kennel of Dandies in the period following the First World War, and by 1938 she had ten Champions in her kennels. Her Ch. Darenth So Wise was a great winner who sired many Champions for her. Some of her original dogs were inclined perhaps to be a little too much on top of their legs instead of being slung between them; this fault was later remedied and generally her stock was considered very sound. Her 'Darenth'-prefixed Dandies: Junerosa, Jeredore, Josse, Janey and Japonique, made a beautiful team of bitches, while the other 'Darenths' Lordy, Penny, Mender, Badger and Good Companion, made a formidable quintet of dogs.

Mrs. Janet Lee Gordon ('Howcaple') was another prominent fancier who maintained a big kennel of some thirty to forty Dandies from 1922 onwards. She had her first Dandie from Mr. J. A. Mather (see Plate 40) about the same time as Mrs. P. Salisbury started in the breed with her Salismore Soloman and Salismore Sheba, also from Mr. Mather. Many of Mather's Dandies were bred from a bitch named Morah and the two referred to were rather light in eye, a common enough failing in the breed about that time in its history. Mrs. Gordon's first champion was Ch. Howcaple Jean by Skilling's Piper. Jean produced a famous daughter, Ch. Howcaple Mustard who produced Ch. Howcaple Mint, later owned by Mrs. McDonnell. Other noted Dandies here were Chs. Howcaple Slioch, Howcaple William, St. Conal's Jess and Howcaple Joanna. Mrs. Gordon can recall the days when the S.D.D.T.C. started and she became secretary. One show run by the club at Tattersall's had an entry of 300! She had a part of the 'Darenth' kennel for a few years, but eventually gave up the really large numbers of dogs. She has been chairman of the club and is now its president. She was a founder member of the W.E.L.K.S. and is now president of that august body —! It is interesting to note that many of the old prefixes appear in the pedigrees of Mrs Gordon's original stock—'Alpin', 'Baillieston', 'Gifford', 'Glassford', 'Glenfarg', 'Matching' and 'St. Conal's'.

L. Irwin Scott, the noted judge and critic, was ever a joy to listen to when discussing Dandies, for he had a wide experience from which to draw. Owning Dandies most of his life, he used the prefix 'Otter' and had a number of good ones including Otter Tuggem and Otter Kiltie to mention only two, but later changed his prefix to 'Camowen' (after the river which flowed through his father's estate and in which he hunted his dogs) when in 1898 his interests changed to Scottish Terriers, and the old 'Otter' prefix was taken over by Mr. Ashmear Bond of Shantallow, Londonderry. Mr. Irwin Scott was a great admirer of Mr. David Baillie of Garbet Hill, Castlecary, who always used a Dandie or two in his hunting teams of sporting dogs. Baillie was an early owner of Border King and the breeder of Fair Janet (32352), Ainsty Tearem (34865) and many others.

Mrs. Phyllis Salisbury's 'Salismore' Dandies are known everywhere. From the time she started with a brace of Dandies from J. A. Mather of Moniaive she has bred cleverly and successfully. She is the best-known breeder of the 'old school' alive today. Her opinion is eagerly sought after and she maintains a very high quality in her stock. Her father kept Dandies although he never exhibited while Mrs. Salisbury commenced showing about 1922. Her first was Salismore Sporran an easy winner of the Dog C.C. at Cruft's that year under Mr. Theo Marples. The dog was bred by George Jardine, Snr in 1920, being by Crab out of Mary Mason, both unregistered Dandies, and was litter brother to J. Millican's Ch. Waterbeck High Water Mark, another mustard. Her kennel was practically wiped out when Salismore Podgy caught distemper at an early show, but one of the survivors was Ch. Salismore Mustard by Salismore Soloman, a dog whose name features in the pedigrees of most present-day Dandies. Since those days Mrs. Salisbury is always campaigning super Dandies to the top honours list. Her latest is a magnificent dog Ch. Salismore Watersend Pioneer and with Salismore Melody and Sweet Lips at the shows, often with their sire, Ch. Salismore Barvae Peppi, she supports the breed well. She had the distinction of gaining the 'Dandie of the Year' award in 1969 with Ch. Salismore Melrose (see Plate 12.) Her kennel is particularly strong in bitches, a policy which has always ensured success. Both Mrs. Salisbury and her daughter, Audrey (Mrs. Hall Parlby), are devotees of the breed and qualified show judges. Mrs. Salisbury has an amazing memory for all that has happened in the breed before and during her association with it. She has kept records for fifty years and maintains a record of some 50,000 names!

George Jardine (Snr) founder of the world-famous 'Waterbeck' kennels in Lockerbie, has a firm niche in the history of the breed. He had his first Dandie from Mr. E. B. Smith's noted strain nearly ninety years ago and owned the dog, Crab. He was successful in popularising the breed and sold two to Mr. Bell-Irving, Master of the Dumfriesshire Otter Hunt. The dogs worked well and eventually went with their master to China. John and George

Jardine, his sons, carried on the noted kennel following their father's death and only this year, the 17th July, 1971, did George pass away. This was a tremendous blow to his family and the breed for he had campaigned many great dogs and supplied with brother John numerous great ones across the Atlantic, where the 'Waterbeck' strain is held in great esteem. George was a championship show judge and one of the breed's keenest fanciers since his return from the war when he had a bad time as a Japanese prisoner of war. John keeps a close eye on the kennel and has been closely associated with his late father in the breed all his life. His uncle John Jardine, now in his eighties is a keen worker too and the family is deeply dyed in Dandie lore. Some wonderful dogs have been bred and reared in Lockerbie, including Chs. Waterbeck Watermark, Waterbeck Welbeck, Weir of Waterbeck, Warrin of Waterbeck and many others. A recent one, Ch. Waterbeck Border Cheer a mustard by Am.Ch. Wassail of Waterbeck has achieved great show successes. Watermark was sold to America, speedily becoming a Champion. A son of his, Am.Ch. Cliffield Larry Langwham, was bred by Miss S. Swift of the 'Cliffield' Dandies. She is an enthusiastic fancier and visitor to shows here and sold Larry to the Jardines in 1957. The late Mr. George Jardine had a highly successful judging trip to the States in September 1968.

An old-timer of the breed who has only recently gone to his rest was Tom Lawson of Lockerbie. He owned the dog, Dryfesdale, and was all his life an enthusiastic fancier of Dandies and in fact all fur and feather. He bred some useful stock, and died in 1955 aged 85 years.

Others who frequented the leading shows and bred some good stock were Mrs. E. H. Bairds ('Bracken'), Mrs. H. M. Dewé ('Handborough'), Mr. R. Powell Williams, who produced an attractive pamphlet on the breed, and Mr. W. Goodall-Copestake, who helped the Dandie Dinmont Terrier Club and prepared a Stud Book and record of the breed for members' use. Also active in the field were Mr. W. Wardlaw Reid, and Mr. John Patrick, who owned Netherby II and judged the breed, and Mr. John Nutsford who judged and kept a large kennel. Mr. E. Berdoe-Wilkinson too was an active member and entered into many discussions which concerned the welfare of the Dandie. Baron

Nugent and his lady of the 'Gally Hill' prefix kept a fairly large kennel of Dandies during the early days of the bench, and campaigned the breed in the south.

The late Mr. H. J. Bidwell, M.V.O., when he was president of the D.D.T.C. composed a song about the Dandie entitled 'The Lay of the Dandie Dinmont Terrier' which was set to music by Mr. W. Berridge-Hicks and published by Mr. T. M. Simpson-Shaw, both words and music being presented to the club by Mrs. Vere Sage. The little ditty entertained many a social evening of the club and the lyric is reproduced here with kind permission of Mrs. Vere Sage. Unfortunately, I cannot reproduce the score.

THE LAY OF THE DANDIE DINMONT TERRIER

You have heard of the sea.
Where they sail so gay and free,
And the sailor with a wife in every port:
And you've heard of soldiers three,
And what pals they used to be,
And how very bravely Tommy Atkins fought.
So to-night I'll sing a song
Of a friend who can't go wrong,
And whose deep affection naught can ever clog.
His love, it far surpasses
The love of lads for lasses,
He's a little Dandie Dinmont Terrier dog.

Chorus:

Sing hey! Sing ho!
He's full of pluck and go,
And for any kind of sport he's very handy,
To hunt is his delight,
From morning until night,
My merry little Border Tyke, my Dandie.
Well! I bought him when a pup.
By myself I trained him up,
And a very clever pupil I have found him.
Rough boys they all deride him,
Declare: 'they can't abide him'
And think 'the bloke wot owns him ought to drown him',
For he's rather quick on boys,
When he hears them make a noise,

And he's very rough on ragged tramps and cadgers.
He hates the kitchen cat,
He never spares a rat,
And he's sudden death on foxes and on badgers.

Chorus:
Sing hey! Sing ho! etc.

He will quickly learn a trick,
Or by your side he'll stick,
And watch you while with your friends you talk.
And he'll quietly guard the home,
But he'll fly if told to come
When 'tis time for us to take our daily walk.
Then for many and many a day,
When after work comes play,
May we search the woods and tramp across the heather;
And when grim death at last
Cries: 'Your earthly days are past',
May we roam in happy hunting grounds for ever.

Chorus:
Sing hey! Sing ho! etc.

3

Modern Exhibitors and Dogs

IN spite of the many restrictions which prevailed here and affected dogdom during the Second World War and the immediate post-war years, the average exhibitor's enthusiasm for his hobby remained undampened. Many of the older Dandie breeders kept the flag flying and with their work and the efforts of fanciers who started in that period, the Dandie Dinmont Terrier was able to keep fairly stable in his popularity.

It is sad to record, however, that a goodly number of the breed's genuine supporters have passed on. In fact, their ranks are sadly depleted and although new breeders have stepped into the Dandie fancy the effect of those gone is one which might well have weakened the breed as a whole. It is not practicable to detail the names of all modern fanciers, their dogs and successes. However, I have mentioned a fair number of leading devotees of the last thirty years and while maintaining some chronological order the script, it has not proved feasible to list the exact dates when each prominent breeder entered or left the breed. I hope, therefore, that you will bear with me in the event of any seeming discrepancies.

The late Misses M. E. and C. H. Ainslie ('Dodrick') had their first Champion in the richly mustard coloured dog Ch. Dodrick Dauntless. He won six C.Cs. in the 1952–4 period. Other C.C. winners owned by the sisters included Dodrick Duchess and Dodrick Drifter. Miss Constance Ainslie, who died as recently as 1969 was a Cruft's judge and committee member of the D.D.T.C.

Miss M. I. B. Baker ('Hayling') before her death, was showing and breeding Dandies from pre-war years and served on the committee of the S.D.D.T.C. Her Ch. Hayling Torquil won twelve C.Cs. and featured in many Brace Class wins with his kennel companion, Ch. Hayling Nettle. Branda of Hayling was another noted inmate of Miss Baker's kennel.

Mrs. I. M. Carlyle ('Dogari') who was so tragically killed in a road accident outside her Sherborne home, bred and exhibited from 1925. She was a well-known judge and exported many Dandies to the U.S.A. Her pepper dog, Ch. Dogari Berkono, was a consistent winner.

Miss C. M. Dandison ('Shrimpney') is highly respected in the breed. The kennel, started by her mother, the late Mrs. M. G. Dandison, achieved much success. Miss Christine Dandison herself has owned the breed since 1926 when she bought a pepper bitch from Miss A. D. Francis ('Rowan') and had her enthusiasm for the Dandie kindled when the famous judge, J. J. Holgate, awarded her first and second prizes with two home-bred 'Shrimpney' bitch youngsters in 1928. She is a Cruft's judge and S.D.D.T.C. committee member. She has owned and bred some superlative stock, including Chs. Shrimpney Sweet Pepper and Shrimpney Sweet Clover. Shrimpney Siren who was whelped during an air-raid got the noted Chs. Shrimpney Sweet William and Shrimpney Sea Shanty. The latter was the sire of Jardine's Chs. Waterbeck Watermark, Waterbeck Wakeful and Waterbeck Warrior. Am. and Can. Ch. Shrimpney Scarlet Star, now owned by Mrs. R. Oliver in California. He has been the top winning Dandie in America during the last few years. Miss Dandison remains very active in the breed, producing first-rate stock in her Stoke Trister kennel.

The late Misses M. E. and C. M. Dickson ('Devadale') will always be remembered for their Dinky Dick, the only tail-male bridge to the celebrated Dirk. They owned Ch. Double Dutch of Devadale and the little mustard bitch, Ch. Diana. This bitch and Ch. Salismore Spice were bred by Mr. R. Sidgwick of Durham from his one Dandie, Ch. Winterton Belle, a daughter of Tommy Dodd. Both ladies judged the breed.

Mrs. A. Jackson ('Minera') does not judge neither does she breed these days. She has owned some noted stock in Chs. Peppercorn of Minera and Whinberry of Minera. Another small kennel which did some useful winning in its day was that of the late Mr. and Mrs. E. Stubbs, whose Ch. Peachum of Wirral, Peachum's Bonna Dee, Perrena Dee, Minna Lou and Sturdy amply demonstrate this kennel's strength in the field.

The renowned 'Bellmead' kennel was founded in 1924 by Miss J. Trefusis Forbes. Later it was taken over by Mrs. C. A. Miles under whose direction the establishment became world famous. Very high-class stock was maintained at all times together with a large and effective stud force which contributed to the breed's welfare. The kennel's first champion was Ch. Bellmead David followed by Chs. Bellmead Defender, Bellmead Seraph and several others including Am.Ch. Bellmead Democrat. Ch. Bellmead Delegate was whelped in 1935 and died in 1949. During his fourteen years he was acclaimed the most outstanding specimen of his breed in the era. He had tremendous character and was a boon as a stud dog. Although his show wins were many and far above average, including eleven C.Cs. under eleven different judges, it is only just to record that his show career was restricted by the shadow of the war years. Had he free rein at stud he might have achieved immense success. He was by the mustard, Messam Tam, out of the pepper, Bellmead Sphinx, and was himself a beautiful badger grey with mustard legs and some tan around the face. Mrs. C. A. Miles picked him from a litter of nine and his breeding was a perfect pedigree blend of all that is considered best from Scottish and southern bloodlines. It went back to such notabilties as Skilling's Piper, Ch. Alpin Stormer, Ch. Glenfarg Chief and a host of others. Delegate sired Ch. Peachum's Wannie Blossom, Salismore Melverley and Chelsfield Donald. Another great dog from these kennels was Bellmead Document who sired Bellmead Declaration from whom stemmed some great winners and Champions. Mrs. C. A. Miles, who was a chairman of the S.D.D.T.C. in her day has now retired. She sold the 'Bellmead' kennel and the famous prefix to Mr. and Mrs. Tom Collier. They have entirely rebuilt the fine kennels and own what can be only described as a model establishment. It is run on highly efficient lines with Dandies an important feature of the establishment. Mr. and Mrs. Collier have campaigned some exceptionally fine specimens through the rings, witness the wonderful Ch. Bellmead Dominion Day and Bellmead Craigvar Callboy who is making his name.

The late Mr. A. H. Lindsay ('Friern') was an experienced dog-fancier and bred Dandies since 1922. He exhibited a good deal, handling Ch. Friern Dandie to win twelve C.Cs. He was a championship show judge of the breed.

Miss D. Miles ('Crooksbury'), although passed on, showed her first Dandie, Hillary Johnny, bred by Miss J. Horsfall in 1930. She judged at championship shows and owned Chs. Hobgoblin's Barnabas, Crooksbury Cloud and Crooksbury Colonist. Miss I. M. F. Murray ('Brynblair') has been breeding and showing useful ones since the last war, her Waterbeck Woodnut being a regular showgoer.

Mrs. H. D. Jameson ('Sowdens') had owned and bred Dandies since the war. She is honorary secretary and treasurer of the S.D.D.T.C. and a noted judge of the breed. She owned the great Ch. Gladsmuir Gay Geisha, one of the famous three litter sisters bred by Fl.-Lt. and Mrs. P. Townshend out of Gladsmuir Gaiety by East Harting Mike. She bred Sowdens Grakle and Brynblair Phoebe, believed by many to be one of the breed's best bitches. Her Sowdens Spartan and Sowdens Hendell Fiona are typical of the high standard she keeps in her kennels and the current great winner, Ch. Sowdens Penelope, with Sowdens Shan and Sowdens Shaun complete the formidable strength of this establishment, which has contributed to Mrs. M. C. Barnett ('Dunkery') with the sensational Ch. Sowdens Speculation. This select kennel is making a strong mark in competition today currently campaigning a number of promising show specimens including Dunkery Vixen and Dunkery Salismore Skylark.

Fl.-Lt. Peter Townshend ('Gladsmuir') and the late Mrs. Millie Townshend referred to above kept Dandies for many years and have contributed extensively to the breed. They bred the three litter sister champions just mentioned and owned the C.C. winner, Salismore Mervyn. Both judged the breed. Fl.-Lt. Townshend married again in 1958 but does not own a breed specimen now, as far as I know.

Mr. S. Marshall ('Leitholm') has been breeding and judging Dandies longer than most people alive today, following on his family tradition in the breed. Mrs. Phyllis Salisbury ('Salismore') bred Ch. Salismore May Queen from a bitch she bought from Mr. Marshall in 1929. Mr. Murray Gate ('Craigvar') started in the breed many years ago and has developed some excellent breeding stock of the right kind. He is a championship show judge and an officer of the D.D.T.C. His prefix figures in many of the breed's leading winners. Miss M. Hunter ('Huntershope') owned the

Dandie Dinmont and his Terriers from a painting by Sir W. Allen, R.A.
Historic Dog Features

W. E. Easton's "Border Queen" (wh. 1877) fro etching by W. Hole
Historic Dog Features

Mr. J. Locke's Dandie Dinmonts "Doctor" and "Tib Mumps" (c. 1878)
Historic Dog Features

Great Terrier Show
Royal Aquarium
April, 3rd 4th & 5th, 1889.

DIPLOMA
AWARDED TO
Mr
Breed
Name
Class №

Humphrey F. de Trafford Presdt Chas Cruft Secty

Reproduction of a Diploma won at Great Terrier Show at the Royal Aquarium in 1889 by Mr. George L. Penrhyn (Mrs. Vere Sage's father) with his Dandie "Little Mustard IV".

A painting by Miss Lucy Waller owned by Mrs. Vere Sage. 1. "Ainsty King" 27723. 2. "Flora McIvor" 19327. 3. "Little Pepper II" 25579. 4. "Raquet" 18592. 5. "Doctor Deans" 25572. 6. "Ainsty Belle" 25595. 7. Ch. "Darkie Deans" 23287. 8. "Davie Deans" 25571. 9. "Victoria Regina" 23348. 10. Ch. "Border King" 16044. 11. Ch. "Heather Peggy" 23326 12. Ch. "Heather Sandy" 23295. 13. (in background) "Ainsty Duchess".

Some of the 'Clane' Dandies: "Headstrong of Clane", "Hazel of Clane", "Busy of Clane", Ch. "Dougal of Clane", "Happy of Clane", Ch. "Hasty of Clane".

James Locke's "Doctor" and Hemming's Bedlington "Geordie" (c. 1879).
Historic Dog Features

Mr. George Jardine, founder of the 'Waterbeck' kennel and Mr. J. B. Richardson ('Slitrig') of Hawick, another pioneer of the breed.

J. A. M. Henderson's "Elmbank Nell".

J. A. M. Henderson's "Glentarky Chief" (wh. 1886).

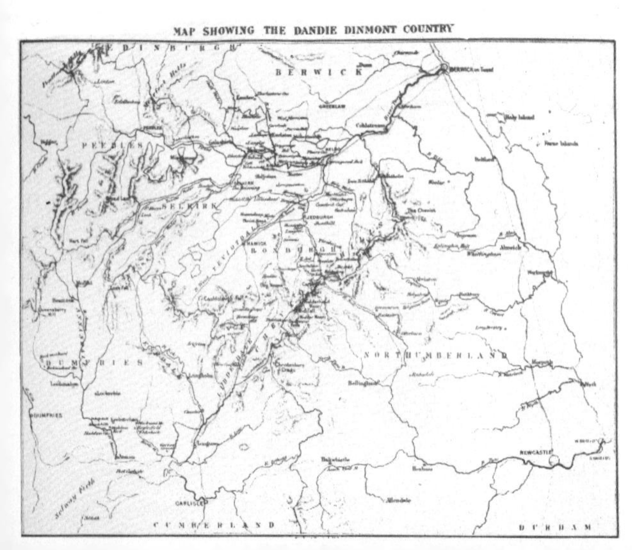

Steel's Ch. "Linnet" (20 lb. pepper) and Ch. "Edenside" (20 lb. mustard) .
Historic Dog Features

T. F. Slater's Ch. "Tweedmouth" (1879).
Historic Dog Features

J. B. Richardson's "Shem" (1870–1883). *Historic Dog Features*

Mr. W. Carrick's Otter Hound "Stanley". *Historic Dog Features*

Mr. W. Carrick's Otter Hound "Lottery". *Historic Dog Features*

"Bellman", an Otter Hound; Pedigree unknown

E. B. Smith's "Podgy II" (1853–1864). *Historic Dog Features*

Mrs. R. Peel Hewitt's Ch. "Tommy Atkins" (34905) from a picture in the possession of Mrs. P. Salisbury. *Historic Dog Features*

"Rough" and "Puck", Dandies. "*Puck*" *bred by Dr. Brown*

Dandie Dinmont Terrier of 1900 as delineated by artist Arthur Wardle. *Historic Dog Features*

"Bandie" (or Bandy) K.C.S.B. Vol. 1. (3039) owned by Rev. W. J. Mellor, also by Capt. P. Lindoe, Bred by Capt. Hamilton. Unknown Pedigree. From a painting by George Earl. *Courtesy of Gerald Massey*

John Alfred Mather of Edinburgh, A
Founder of the D.D.T.C. and owner
of "Dr. Syntax". *Historic Dog Feature.*

F. A. B. Coupland's "Border Prince" (KCSB. 13,815) a 23 lb. pepper *Historic Dog Features*

P. S. Lang's "Pepper" (1856–1871) *Historic Dog Features*

bitch, Ch. Gigha of Cruan, and bred some useful winners including the noted late Ch. Huntershope Cutty Sark, owned by Mrs. J. A. Watt('Cruan'), a lady who has been breeding and showing for the past thirty years. She bred the pepper bitch, Ch. Gigha of Cruan, and also Cruan Viking, the sire of Ch. Glassford Curate. The late Mr. Watt was editor of the D.D.T.C. *Magazine*. Mr. J. Johnston ('Sykemoor') died in 1958 but he and his son were showing Dandies since the war, owning Ch. Gladsmuir Gay Goddess and serving on the D.D.T.C. committee.

Mr. R. Smith is a championship show judge and still attends the Carlisle shows, being a very keen supporter. He had Pride of Pleasley, a C.C. winner bred by Dr. J. A. Wilson ('Glassford'). Mrs. E. M. H. Oldham ('Coneygreave') started in the breed before the start of war. She died some two decades ago but her breeding is effective in Waterbeck Wakeful also in Coneygreave Maharajah whose names feature in many pedigrees.

Miss I. Paterson ('Franabella') has always had Dandies. She bred and owned Ch. Franabella Cinders from which she bred Franabella Madrigal, owned then by Surgeon Vice-Admiral Sir Alexander Ingleby-Mackenzie, C.B., K.St.J., and exhibited often by Lady Ingleby-Mackenzie who won a reserve C.C. with her at Carlisle in 1958. Cinders is now dead and Miss Paterson, a championship show judge, has been instrumental in helping many a novice exhibitor.

Mrs. Vere Sage ('Clane') is well-known in the Dandie world. Her prefix figures strongly in modern winners. She attended shows many years ago with her mother Mrs. Leycester Penrhyn from Ireland and a diploma won by her father George L. Penrhyn with Little Mustard IV at The Great Terrier Show Royal Aquarium in 1889 is illustrated in this book (see Plate 20). She had Chs. Sandy of Clane and Hillary Timothy among her many winners and exhibited Hamish, Hasty and Happy, all 'of Clane' with considerable success. She is a judge of the breed.

Miss M. E. Vernon ('Weatheroak') started after the war and owned some effective stock, her Little Boy Blue of Weatheroak being a well-known show winner. Miss G. Wise ('Hergaden') has been in the breed a long time and is responsible for breeding some excellent stock including Hergaden Hallow-een, Hergaden Robert and Hergaden Harvest. The first-named dog sired Mrs. V. Sage's winning litter. As far as I am aware, Miss Wise judges seldom to-day and does not own a Dandie at present. Miss C. M. Francis ('Higham') is another who has been in Dandies for many years. She is a championship show judge and had her first dog, Joffre, as long ago as 1916. Later, with Higham Judith bought through Major Hope of Allerly in 1921 she bred, among others, Higham Joy, a mustard by Ch. Alpin Raider.

The late Miss Rhoda Whitelaw ('Hatton') was a figurehead in the breed. She commenced exhibiting in the early thirties, doing much of her initial winning with Alpin Waes Me and Alpin Mab. She bred some fine stock including Chs. Hatton Revina, Relinda, Reina, Roseleaf, Red Gleam and Navigator. She had also Ch. Merry Muse (bred by Mr. R. Tait) and herself bred the noted Ch. Hatton Redcap who won no less than seventeen C.Cs. and was Best in Show at the Scottish Kennel Club shows in 1957. The same year he went Best in Show at Perth, Best Terrier at Bath Championship Show and won extensively elsewhere. He was also 'Dandie of the Year' in 1956 and 1957. Miss Whitelaw was chairman of the D.D.T.C. and a generous supporter of the breed. She judged in America in 1952. Her Ch. Hatton Nimrod by Ch. Hatton Nimbus was her current winner, gaining his title just before she died.

Mr. A. Kennedy, B.Sc., M.R.C.V.S. ('Kenriva') is a great advocate of the working Dandie as well as being a championship show judge. He is Hon. Veterinary Surgeon to the D.D.T.C. Miss R. Bradbury ('Watersend') a Cruft's judge and S.D.D.T.C. committee member, made her initial contact with the breed at 'Bellmead' about 1933. She bred Ch. Sage of Watersend, Catmint of Watersend and owned Ch. Shrimpney Sweet Clover. Her game little Ch. Watersend Magic died in 1970 but in her hey-day was never unplaced in competition. Miss Bradbury campaigned Ch. Shrimpney Sweet Clover to her title. The bitch was a grand-daughter of her old Red Peppers, the kennel's first home-bred winner in 1937. In the fifties she made up Ch. Shrimpney Signet and Ch. Winnie of Clane. The noted Ch. Salismore Watersend Pioneer she bred, is owned by Mrs. Phyllis Salisbury.

Mrs. H. M. Gilbert, formerly Miss Jones of Kettering, owned the nice dog, Salismore Shem, before her marriage and did well with him at the shows. Today, she remains a keen adherent to the breed and has in fact, just purchased a new puppy to recommence activities in it. Lord Melgund ('Minto') is president of the D.D.T.C. today—his grandfather was the club's first president when it was inaugurated at Selkirk in 1875.

Mrs. A. Woolf ('Woolo') does not show or breed these days, but she owned and bred Ch. Wadi and maintained some good specimens in her kennel. The late Mrs. Anne Nairn Walker ('Fruach') bred some good ones in the fifties including Ch. Fruach Toby (seven C.Cs.), Ch. Fruach Morna (four C.Cs.) and Ch. Fruach Kirstie (six C.Cs.). When she died in 1952 she had decreed that all her dogs were to be put down. This was a sad loss to the breed and all but wound up the 'S.A.' ('Shamrock-Abbotsford') Line. Mr. Robert Tait had no prefix but had been a Dandie owner all his life. He bred Ch. Merry Muse and some good winners, but seldom exhibited, dying in 1954.

Miss G. Saunders was in residence at 'Bellmead' since that kennels' foundation. She is very well-known to all the old-timers and has judged at S.D.D.T.C. shows. She is retired now in Littlehampton, but her memory of the Dandies and their owners in her time is exceptional. Mrs. V. McKie, late sister of Sir Oswald Mosley bred some useful stock in her 'Glencaird' kennel and Mrs. A. Moir (formerly Mrs. B. Fry) was a noted championship show judge before she retired from the breed. Her Falinge Jane was well-known and she owned Cookie of Clane bred by Mrs. Leycester Penrhyne.

Miss F. E. Soutter and Miss M. E. Greenlees ('Drevaburn') since the demise of George Jardine, owner of the big 'Waterbeck' kennel, have now what is probably the largest kennels in Scotland. Their first dog, Dodrick Dazzler, was a pepper purchased from Miss C. H. Ainslie. Foundation bitches were obtained from Miss C. Dandison (Shrimpney Slipper Satin) and Mrs. P. Salisbury (Salismore Pennywise). The latter bitch has so far produced three champions, the litter sisters, Chs. Salismore Scattercash, Drevaburn Ardailsa and Drevaburn Falloch. Their Drevaburn Jocktie and Jamie are at stud and Drevaburn Gigha has shown her worth. Their original stud dog, Cockdurno Comet of Drevaburn, was bred by Mr. and Mrs. Alick Buchanan-Smith. These two ladies produce the D.D.T.C.'s *Magazine* with great efficiency.

Miss Mary T. Carr ('Warkworth') has had Dandies for many

years and runs her successful show kennel alongside the Coquet Water in Northumberland. Mrs. Ann Cowen ('Durranhill') is related by marriage to the Jardines and has produced some sound and typical stock. She is a keen breed supporter. Mr. and Mrs. H. Drury ('Culston') are enthusiastic exhibitors and maintain stock of excellent quality. Mr. J. Fox ('Wizaburn') has bred some good ones, Mrs. B. Sullivan's late Ch. Dandyhow Wizaburn Vixen being notable. Mrs. Sullivan ('Dandy How') is a breed judge and is a committee member of the S.D.D.T.C. She is well known for her Border Terriers too. Mrs. Peggy Hulme ('Hendell') trained under Mrs. C. A. Miles at 'Bellmead' in the Haslemere days and had her own first Dandie in 1942. This was a winner named Newlandshaw Sakes. Well-versed in dogs generally, with veterinary as well as breeding and exhibiting knowledge she can claim for her dogs no less than twenty-two C.Cs. She states that she owes Mrs. C. A. Miles and the late H. S. Lloyd ('of Ware') much for their help in her training when she started. Later she became head kennelmaid at 'Bellmead' in Old Windsor, owning Chs. Bellmead Sunburst, Dogari Carafe, Hendell Pippin, Hendell Pocket Prince and Int. Ch. Hendell Colislinn Loelia.

Miss M. Mellis ('Gardenside') has spent a good time abroad, but has had Dandies in her family since childhood, the first being a 'Fruach' dog named Piper. At the commencement of the last war she purchased from George Sleigh a mustard bitch and bred from her. Later with two 'Waterbeck' bitches she continued her interest and from one of these bitches produced her well-known Ash of Gardenside, by Bellmead Delphic. He presides as grandsire of Ch. Bawbee of Gardenside and Alpheus and Broom of 'Gardenside', both these being at stud. Miss Mellis is chairman of the S.D.D.T.C. and a Member of The Kennel Club. Mrs. M. L. Chandler's Gossip of Gardenside is making a mark in the breed and this is another of Miss Mellis' breeding. Mrs. Chandler is a most enthusiastic exhibitor and with having a bitch of this type and character to work with must be very satisfying. Mrs. P. A. Mattinson ('Senacre') does well at the shows with her home-bred stock and her Senacre Lollipop is certainly a pleasing Dandie. The late Mrs. Anne Penny ('Kitewood') judged the breed and bred a number of winners in her many years with the breed. The best-known of these were Ch. Kitewood Ragamuffin and her pepper daughter,

Ch. Bellmead Gypsy of Kitewood. Another long-standing exhibitor is Mrs. W. Seymour-Stevenson ('Twinkling'). Her Colislinn Soulful of Twinkling and Wendella of Waterbeck are regular attenders at the specialist events.

Miss C. E. Graham and her sister at Harrow no longer breed Dandies, although they were very keen in their day. They bred the Author's pepper bitch, Bandits Belle Beaver. She did some winning, then was sold to Mr. Brian Peel Yates ('Danaff') who died in 1967 after a long illness. His Ch. Danaff Debut and Danaff Doran were popular and successful winners at the shows.

MAIN LINES

Today the 'O.G.' ('Old Ginger') Line stands pre-eminent. From the main stem at the point where appears John Skilling's Piper two branches emanate, both from Piper's sons—Dr. Syntax and Ch. Giffnock Pedlar. The former in association with Mrs. P. Salisbury's Salismore Soloman, the latter with Mrs. Leycester Penrhyn's Sandie of Clane. The 'O.G.' Line is now far less forcefully represented than it was and has really little more for breed students than antiquarian interest. The 'S.A.' Line ('Shamrock–Abbotsford') from which the 'S.S.' Line ('Shamrock–Shem') had its source are tail-male virtually dried up. The old subsidiary Lines, i.e. 'H.B.' ('Heather Badger') and 'D' ('Dirk') and probably defunct.

THE 'O.G.' LINE

This Line, although rather slow to establish itself in the two decades following the First World War, can claim a more lasting benefit in its effect upon the breed. Through Mr. W. Poole's Charlie (16935), whose dam was a tail-male descendant of Stoddart's saddleback dog, Old Dandie I, a breed foundation stone, some twenty-one Champions were produced in that period. Charlie sired Mr. G. A. B. Leatham's mustard brace, Chs. Heather Peggy and Heather Sandy. Sandy sired Ch. Ainsty Dandie, sire of Ch. Cannie Lad and Mr. T. B. Potterton's Ch. Puff, sire of Mrs. K. Spencer's Ch. Braw Lad.

Old Ginger himself was a son of the Fifth Duke of Buccleuch's foundling dog, Old Pepper, and on his dam's side bred from Sir

Walter Scott's famous Terriers. Ch. Bellmead Delegate and the pepper bitch, Ch. Bellmead Seraph, Ch. Darenth Lordy, Ch. Messan Giles, Ch. Hillary Timothy and the mustard bitch, Ch. Howcaple Joanna—all are descended tail-male from him.

Skilling's Piper, born in 1914, was responsible for putting new life in the Line through his two sons Doctor Syntax and Andrew MacCulloch's Ch. Giffnock Pedlar and the Hon. Mrs. S. McDonnell's Ch. Darenth Shian. It is interesting to record that from this section of the breed's bloodlines Ch. Waterbeck High Water Mark is the only Champion who does not come through Skilling's Piper. The Line at the time was particularly strong in the production of good mustards.

THE 'S.A.' LINE

The dog, Shamrock (3089), born in 1866 and owned by the Rev. S. Tenison Mosse, claims descent through Francis Somner's Shem, a 14-lb pepper born in 1839, from Sir Walter Scott's and James Davidson's Terriers. Mrs. Phyllis Salisbury has seen a rough sketch of this blue dog, and describes him as lacking the true classical outline of the typical Dandie, but very strongly made with great bone and feet, in fact a most workmanlike dog, amply coated.

He got two noted sons in Abbotsford born in 1872, and J. B. Richardson's (Dumfries) grey-and-tan Shem, born in 1870. Richardson's Shem, a 19-lb dog, was responsible for the Shamrock–Shem or 'S.S.' Line. He did not prove a very prolific sire, producing Mr. T. F. Slater's controversial Ch. Tweedmouth, born 1879, a badly overshot specimen who would not have achieved a show title these days. However, Shem had some useful lineal descendants, among them the outstanding bitch, Ch. Ancrum Fanny, a pepper owned by Mrs. Lloyd Rayner born in 1894. This bitch was thought by the late Irwin Scott to be the best Dandie he had ever seen and judged. Mr. E. W. H. Blagg's mustard, Ch. Kyber, born in 1893 and Ch. Scotland Prince (1227B), a dog very famous in his day, but who appears very short and straight in back from his picture. This dog was owned by Mr. R. W. Robertson of Jedburgh, popularly known as 'Bobby the Bellman'. A more modern representative of the Line was the pepper, Bellmead Darroch.

Abbotsford on the other hand did much for the prestige of the 'S.A.' Line in that he produced a descendancy responsible during the twenty-year period between the wars for twenty-four dog Champions and twenty-one bitch Champions. These totalled over half the outstanding Dandies of the period. Through Abbotsfords descendant Ch. Border King (16044) born in 1882 came most of Shamrock's lineal stock, among them Mr. George Shiel's Ch. Thistle Grove Dargai, born in 1903, and Mrs. T. Simpson Shaw's famous 'Alpin, Chs. Stormer, Slitrig, Lochinvar, Roro, Oracle and Catkin and the lovely bitch, Bonnie Lassie, who was best Terrier at Cruft's, 1902.

The little mustard, Ch. Alpin Raider (1309CC), born in 1920 produced a number of great ones, including the Hon. Mrs. S. McDonnel's Ch. Darenth So Wise (120FF) and his grandson, Mrs. P. Salisbury's Ch. Salismore Sovereign (1733MM), a Dandie of extraordinary quality, character and beauty.

Another noted son of Raider was Ch. Alpin Oberon (1458MM) born in 1930, who sired in his turn a number of Champion dogs and bitches. This dog had an exceptionally good head, reminiscent of the true Dandie as drawn by artists nearly a century previously. Every generation descended tail-mail from Ch. Thistle Grove Dargai has provided at least one Champion to represent the 'S.A.' Line and many modern entries in the *Kennel Club Stud Book* can be traced back to him.

THE 'H.B.' LINE

This Line owes its source to a pepper dog of unknown lineage called Heather Badger (39378) owned about 1895 by Mr. Robert Chapman, the great Scottie pioneer. This dog is the tail-male ancestor of a number of Champion dogs and bitches including the famous post-war Ch. Friern Dandie (409CC). This celebrated post-war winner sired the pepper brothers, Ch. Potford Plunderer (532FF) and Ch. Potford Highlander (129GG), and is in the pedigrees of many modern Dandies. Unfortunately, it is difficult to be precise about Heather Badger as there were two or three dogs contemporary with him, all bearing the same name.

THE 'D' LINE

This Line is reproduced by Mr. E. Bradshaw Smith's Dirk. His blood passes through to such famous dogs as Ch. Otter, Ch. Blacket House Yet, Ch. Graythwaite Jock and a number of other noted winners shown on the chart.

Champion Bitches of the Original 'O.G.' Line

*Ch. Heather Peggy	by	Charlie (W. Pool's)
*Ch. Milverton Duchess	by	Ch. Braw Lad
Ch. Katrine Teaser	by	Ch. Canny Lad
*Ch. Katrine Fairy	by	Ch. Canny Lad
Ch. Gordon Daisy	by	Gordon Sandy
Ch. Ossington Maid	by	Border Dick
Ch. Valclusa Duchess	by	Camowen Hero
Ch. Giffnock Gin	by	Cairnside Wonder
Ch. Howcaple Jean	by	Piper (J. Skilling's)
Ch. St. Conal's Jess	by	Piper (J. Skilling's)
Ch. Darenth Jyllis	by	Ch. Giffnock Pedlar
Ch. Waterbeck High Watermark	by	Crab
Ch. Salismore Mustard	by	Salismore Soloman
Ch. Darenth Japonique	by	Camowen Cobbler
*Ch. Howcaple Joanna	by	Timothy of Clane
Ch. Darenth Jina	by	Timothy of Clane
Ch. Bellmead Seraph	by	Ch. Darenth Mender
*Ch. Salismore Melverley	by	Ch. Bellmead Delegate
Ch. Shrimpney Sweet Pepper	by	Ch. Bellmead Delegate
Ch. Shrimpney Sweet Clover	by	Bellmead Declaration
*Ch. Peachum's Bonna Dee	by	Shrimpney Siren
Ch. Gladsmuir Goldilocks	by	Bellmead Document
Ch. Fruach Kirstie	by	Chelsfield Donald
Ch. Fruach Morna	by	Chelsfield Donald
Ch. Crooksbury Cloud	by	Ch. Hobgoblin's Barnabas
*Ch. Bellmead Frost	by	Bellmead Declaration
Ch. Hayling Nettle	by	Mustard of Hayling
Ch. Peachum's Minna Lou	by	Ch. Hayling Torquil
Ch. Whinberry of Minera	by	Trump Card of Twinkling
Ch. Peachum's Perenna Dee	by	Shepherds Commander
Ch. Merry Muse	by	Waterbeck Watermark
Ch. Franabella Cinders	by	Bellmead Dynamic
*Ch. Salismore Parsley	by	Bellmead Declaration
Ch. Glassford Clementina	by	Waterbeck Watermark
*Ch. Gladsmuir Gay Geisha	by	Bellmead Declaration
Ch. Gladsmuir Gay Garland	by	Bellmead Declaration

Ch. Gladsmuir Gay Goddess	by	Bellmead Declaration
*Ch. Salismore Peasblossom	by	Bellmead Delphic
Ch. Glassford Diadem	by	Waterbeck Watermark
Ch. Pride of Pleasley	by	Waterbeck Warrin

* Probably the best

The following Dandies have won C.Cs. during the 1959–71 period in the Lines shown

'O.G.' Line—Dr. Syntax Branch

Ch. Hendel Pocket Prince	by	Hendell Bellmead Daring
Ch. Salismore Barvae Peppi	by	Glassford Marksman
Ch. Bellmead Dominion Day	by	Ch. Culston Ambassador
Ch. Salismore Melrose	by	Hendell Bellmead Daring
Ch. Sowdens Speculation	by	Ch. Salismore Moreton or Shrimpney Scarlet Stripe
Sowdens Spartan	by	Ch. Salismore Barvae Peppi
Dunkery Salismore Skylark	by	Salismore Strathspey
Ch. Salismore Watersend Pioneer	by	Hendell Huckleberry
Hendell Redwood	by	Ch. Salismore Barvae Peppi
Drevaburn Jocktie	by	Ch. Hendell Pocket Prince
Drevaburn Jamie	by	Ch. Hendell Pocket Prince
Ch. Bellmead Sunburst	by	Bellmead Dauntless
Ch. Bellmead Gypsey of Kitewood	by	Hendell Bellmead Daring
Salismore Monybuie	by	Ch. Salismore Barvae Peppi
Povey's Sweet Briar	by	Bellmead Delectus

'O.G.' Line—Giffnock Pedlar/Sandy of Clane Branch

Ch. Tawny Owl of Weatheroak	by	Ch. Redwing of Hatton
Ch. Sage of Watersend	by	Ch. Shrimpney Sweet William
Ch. Sowdens Penelope	by	Ch. Shrimpney Short Circuit
Ch. Shrimpney Sunstar	by	Shrimpney Short Statement
Ch. Shrimpney Signet	by	Shrimpney Scarlet Stripe
Ch. Salismore Scattercash	by	Ch. Wizaburn Destiny
Ch. Kitewood Ragamuffin	by	Ch. Shrimpney Signet
Ch. Hendell Pippin	by	Ch. Redwing of Hatton
Ch. Hendell Colislinn Loelia	by	Ch. Red Gleam of Hatton
Ch. Glassford Whin	by	Ch. Shrimpney Short Circuit
Ch. Glassford Musk	by	Glassford Dirk

Ch. Glassford Craigvar Covergirl	by	Ch. Shrimpney Short Circuit
Ch. Bawbee of Gardenside	by	Shrimpney Silver Penny
Ch. Drevaburn Falloch	by	Ch. Hatton Nimbus
Ch. Drevaburn Ardailsa	by	Ch. Wizaburn Destiny
Ch. Dandyhow Wizaburn Vixen	by	Ch. Wizaburn Destiny
Ch. Hatton Nimrod	by	Ch. Hatton Nimbus
Ch. Waterbeck Border Cheer	by	Am.Ch. Wassail of Waterbeck
Shrimpney Starry Night	by	Shrimpney Scarlet Stripe
Ch. Salismore Parasol	by	Ch. Salismore Proctor
Ch. Salismore Mermaid	by	Ch. Salismore Silversand

Some Notable Bitches of the 'S.A.' Line of the current era

Salismore Mischief	by	Salismore Swordsman
Sowdens Shan	by	Sowdens Shaun
Sowdens Hendell Fiona	by	Sowdens Highlight
Gossip of Gardenside	by	Sowdens Shaun
Salismore Pensive	by	Salismore Swordsman

Champion Bitches of the 'S.A.' Line

Ch. Elspeth	by	Border Viper
Ch. Bonnie Lassie	by	Black Adder
Ch. Giffnock Ferrit	by	Giffnock Rag
Ch. Colvend Nell	by	Urr Tam
Ch. Allerley Bee	by	Ch. Alpin Slitrig
Ch. Scotby Daisy	by	Scotby Jim
Ch. Diana	by	Macheath
Ch. Ellwyn Belle	by	Loyal Leyden
Ch. Potford Braw Lassie	by	Blue Rock
Ch. Hazlewood Meg	by	Ch. Thistlegrove Dargai
Ch. Uppa	by	Kenspeckle
Ch. Jovial Jenny	by	Dunion
Ch. Gordon Daisy	by	Tartan Sandy
Ch. Dark Dame of Priorwood	by	Ch. Tommy Dodd
Ch. Darenth Jill	by	Alpin Davie
Ch. Clarach Meg	by	Ch. Alpin Raider
Ch. Rowan Minna	by	Matching Rory
Ch. Howcaple Mustard	by	Matching Rory
Ch. Darenth Janey	by	Ch. Darenth So Wise
Ch. Darenth Josse	by	Ch. Darenth So Wise

Ch. Kirkside Jessica	by	Salismore Murdoch
Ch. Darenth Janibel	by	Ch. Alpin Oberon
Ch. Alpin Catkin	by	Ch. Alpin Oberon
Ch. Howcaple Slioch	by	Ch. Alpin Oberon
Ch. Darenth Junerosa	by	Darenth Wisdom
Ch. Darenth Jeredore	by	Darenth Wisdom
Ch. Towser	by	Slitrig Rob Roy
Ch. Clydewsdale Jean	by	Scotby Dan
Ch. Joycelyn of Casith	by	Ch. Wadi
Ch. Salismore Sassoline	by	Am.Ch. Bellmead Democrat
Ch. Darenth Jacmint	by	Ch. Howcaple Mint
Ch. Hatton Revina	by	Hatton Rust
Ch. True Blue of Twinkling	by	Mr. Deeds of Devadale
Ch. Hatton Relinda	by	Mr. Deeds of Devadale
Ch. Gigha of Cruan	by	Cruan Charles

Some Champion Bitches from the old 'D' (Dirk) Line

*Ch. Oak Apple	by	Ch. Blacket House Yet
*Ch. Giffnock Luna	by	Ch. Maxwelton Barney
*Ch. Milverton Lady	by	Kelso Scout
Ch. Giffnock Twilight	by	Giffnock Smuggler
Ch. Double Dutch of Devadale	by	Dinkey Dick
Ch. Peppercorn of Minera	by	Dinkey Dick
Ch. Blitz	by	Grip (5560)
Ch. Laird	by	Grip (5560)
*Ch. Border Queen	by	Davie (Redford's)

* Probably the best

Some Champion Bitches from the old 'H.B.' (Heather Badger) Line

*Ch. Salismore Spice	by	Ch. Glenfarg Chief
Ch. Salismore May Queen	by	Rowan Bruce
Ch. Glassford Kathie	by	Glassford Jock

* Outstanding bitch

Some Champion bitches from the old 'S.S.' (Shamrock–Shem) Line

Ch. Maid of Rathan	by	Ch. Thistle Dandie
Ch. Kelso Yet	by	Thistlegrove Tinker
Ch. Evina	by	Hawick Gallant
*Ch. Ancrum Fanny	by	Ancrum Pearl II

* Outstanding bitch

The 'O.G.' ('Old Ginger') Line

- Old Pepper (Foundling) 5th Duke of Buccleuch
  - OLD GINGER (E. B. Smith)
    - Dandie (L) (E. B. Smith)
      - Boxer (E. B. Smith)
        - Tuggem (Rev. McMorland and E. B. Smith)
          - Charlie (W. Pool)
            - Red Angus
              - Daryll
                - Bruce (John Flynn)
                  - Donald (John Skilling)
                    - Piper (John Skilling)
                      - Dr. Syntax (J. A. Mather)
                        - Salismore Soloman
                          - Ch. Darenth Shian
                            - Ch. Darenth Lordy
                              - Salismore Major
                                - Messan Tam
                                  - Ch. Bellmead Delegate
                                    - Chelsfield Donald
                                      - Fruach Heath
                                        - Ch. Dodrick Dauntless
                                    - Bellmead Decision
                                      - Bellmead Domino
                                    - Bellmead Document
                                      - Bellmead Declaration
                                        - Ch. Grainsby Squire
                                        - Ch. Bellmead Dominant
                                      - Ch. Dogari Berkono
                                    - Salismore Pikeman
                                      - Ch. Peachems Sturdy
                                  - Ch. Messan Giles
                                    - Red Peppers
                            - Ch. Darenth Penny
                              - Ch. Peachum of Wirral
                              - Camowen Coleman
                                - Waterbeck Golden Flake
                                  - Goldfinder
                                    - Coneygreave Maharajah
                                      - Ch. Hobgoblins Barnabas
                                        - Ch. Hayling Torquil
                                          - Bellmead Delphic
                      - Ch. Giffnock Pedlar
                        - Ch. Potford Pibrock
                        - Sandie of Clane
                          - Camowen Cobbler
                            - Ch. Darenth Mender
                          - Timothy of Clane
                            - Ch. Gart-connel Andrew
                            - Darenth Christopher Robin
                              - Ch. Darenth Good Companion
                                - East Harting Colin
                                  - Shimpney Siren
                                    - Ch. Shrimpney Sweet William
                                      - Ch. Sage of Watersend
                                    - Shimpney Sea Shanty
                                      - Ch. Waterbeck Watermark
                                        - Ch. Salismore Silversand
                                        - Hatton Rockie
                                          - Ch. Hatton
                                      - Ch. Weir of Waterbeck
                                      - Waterbeck Wakeful
                                        - Shrimpney Sweet Pickle
                                          - Ch. Crooksbury Colonist
                                      - Ch. Waterbeck Welbeck
                                      - Water-beck Warrin
                            - Ch. Hillary Timothy
              - Red Gauntlet
                - Crusader
                  - Keepsake
                    - Lockerbie Bruce
                      - Bruce
                        - Crab
              - Red Murdoch
                - Gordon Sandy
            - Ch. Heather Sandy
              - Ch. Anstey Dandy
                - Ch. Puff
                  - Ch. Braw Lad
                - Ch. Canine Lad
            - Young Charlie II
              - Bold
                - Border Dick
                  - Thistle Grove Mischief
                    - Ch. Rannoch Mohr
                  - Cargen Prince
                    - Cairnside Wonder
            - Little Charlie
              - Bob III
                - Little Kerr
                  - Camowen Hero

('Shamrock-Abbotsford') Line

- Puck (Dr. Brown)
  - Brandy (J. Scott)
    - Pepper (J. Scott)
      - Mustard (Hodges) wh. 1852
        - SHAMROCK wh. 1866
          - ABBOTSFORD wh. 1872
            - Badger 6636
              - Ch. Border King
                - Mac Siccar
                  - Giffnock Tinker
                    - Giffnock Rag
                  - Little Rodger
                    - Little Jim
                      - **Urr Ben**
                        - Ch. Thistle Grove Dargai
                          - Melgund Hero
                            - Bobbie
                              - **Ch.** Sunstar
                          - Loyal Leyden
                          - Ch. Gordon Prince
                          - Ch. Tommy
                            - Ch. Tommy Dodd
                              - **Ch.** Ellwyn Kith
                              - **Ch.** Moathill Tinker
                                - West View Laddie
                                  - Ch. Anson Asome
                            - Ch. Alpin Stormer
                              - Ch. Rowan Warrior
                              - Alpin Davie
                                - Ch. Alpin Raider
                                  - Ch. Darenth So Wise
                                    - Ch. Darenth Badger
                                      - Ch. Salismore Sovereign
                                    - Darenth Wisdom
                                      - Ch. Howcaple William
                                        - Ranger William
                                          - Future Fame Bentam Scamper
                                            - Kaspar of Cruan
                                              - Cruan Charles
                                  - Ch. Burpham Jock
                                    - Burpham Rusty
                                      - James of Casta Ch. Wadi
                                        - Ch. Joe of Castisa
                                    - Burpham Andra
                                      - Slitrig Rob Roy
                                    - Ch. Simple Jinks
                                  - Ch. Alpin Oracle
                                    - Ch. Alpin Roro
                                  - Ch. Alpin Oberon
                                    - Ch. Bellmead Defender
                                      - Am. Ch. Bellmead Democrat
                                    - Ch. Howcaple Mint
                                    - Ch. Guestling Quince
                                    - Ch. Alpin Osiris
                                    - Fruach Michael
                                      - Ch. Fruach Toby
                                    - Alpin Waes Me
                                      - Hatton Rust
                        - Urr Rab
                          - Ch. Rathan Lad
                        - Thistle Grove Ben
                          - Ch. Alpin Slitrig
                            - Ch. Alpin Lochinvar
                        - Urr Tam
                        - Ch. Cargen Pilot
                          - Ch. Cairnside Best
                            - Ch. Brawny Kim
                              - Macheath
                            - Scotby Jim
                              - Ch. Scotby Tip Top
                                - Blue Rock
                                - Scotby Badger
                                  - Scotby Dan
                                    - Southboro' Sternmarch
                                      - Ch. Huckleberry Helmsman
                                      - Salismore Murdoch
                - Ch. Tartan King
                  - Tartan Sandy
                - Border Viper
                  - Tartan Sandy
                - Border Chief
                  - What's Wanted
                    - Kenspeckle
                      - Bobby the Bellman
                        - Dunion

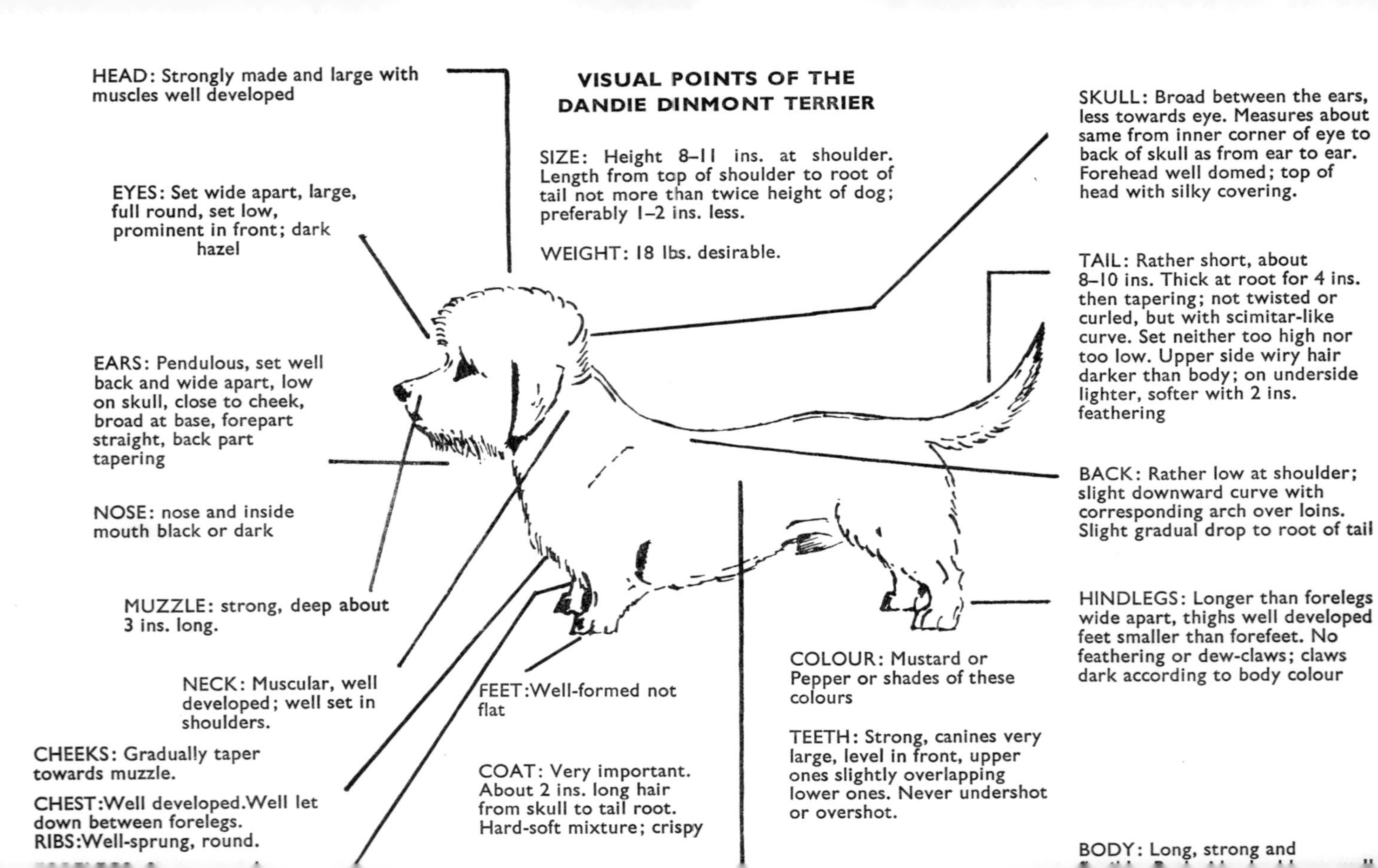
VISUAL POINTS OF THE
DANDIE DINMONT TERRIER
HEAD: Strongly made and large with muscles well developed
EYES: Set wide apart, large, full round, set low, prominent in front; dark hazel
EARS: Pendulous, set well back and wide apart, low on skull, close to cheek, broad at base, forepart straight, back part tapering
NOSE: nose and inside mouth black or dark
MUZZLE: strong, deep about 3 ins. long.
NECK: Muscular, well developed; well set in shoulders.
CHEEKS: Gradually taper towards muzzle.
CHEST: Well developed. Well let down between forelegs.
RIBS: Well-sprung, round.
SIZE: Height 8–11 ins. at shoulder. Length from top of shoulder to root of tail not more than twice height of dog; preferably 1–2 ins. less.
WEIGHT: 18 lbs. desirable.
FEET: Well-formed not flat
COAT: Very important. About 2 ins. long hair from skull to tail root. Hard-soft mixture; crispy
COLOUR: Mustard or Pepper or shades of these colours
TEETH: Strong, canines very large, level in front, upper ones slightly overlapping lower ones. Never undershot or overshot.
SKULL: Broad between the ears, less towards eye. Measures about same from inner corner of eye to back of skull as from ear to ear. Forehead well domed; top of head with silky covering.
TAIL: Rather short, about 8–10 ins. Thick at root for 4 ins. then tapering; not twisted or curled, but with scimitar-like curve. Set neither too high nor too low. Upper side wiry hair darker than body; on underside lighter, softer with 2 ins. feathering
BACK: Rather low at shoulder; slight downward curve with corresponding arch over loins. Slight gradual drop to root of tail
HINDLEGS: Longer than forelegs wide apart, thighs well developed feet smaller than forefeet. No feathering or dew-claws; claws dark according to body colour
BODY: Long, strong and

4
The Standard

THE Dandie Dinmont Terrier Club can justly claim to have been one of the first specialist clubs for pedigree dogs. Only the Bulldog Club and the Bedlington Terrier Club are older in canine history—and then only by a relatively narrow margin. The first meeting of the Dandie Dinmont Terrier Club was held at Selkirk in the Fleece Hotel on the 17th November, 1875. The founders of this club were present or represented at the meeting, and it is of interest to record their names—President, Lord Melgund, Minto House, Hawick; vice-president, Mr. P. S. Lang of Selkirk; hon. joint secretaries and treasurers, Mr. Hugh Dalziel,* Greenhill House, Harlesden Glen, London, and Mr. Wm. Strachan* of Linlithgow.

The founder members Messrs. J. Brough (Carlisle), J. C. Carrick* (Carlisle), Wm. Carrick Jnr.* (Carlisle), Matthew Charlton* (Browndeanlaws, Jedburgh), George Coulthard* (Carlisle), W. E. Easten* (Hull), Adam Elliott (Semieston, Jedburgh), Joseph Finchett* (Llanrwst, Wales), William Foster* (Carlisle), Joseph Heywood* (Bangor), Gerard Leatham* (Thorganby Hall, York), James Locke (Selkirk), John Alfred Mather* (Edinburgh), J. Miller (Rosebank, Moffat), The Rev. S. Tenison Mosse* of Great Smeaton Rectory, Northallerton, G. Park (Galashiels), George Parker* (Riddell, Selkirk), James Patterson (Rutherford, Kelso), W. Poole* (Dumfries), Wm. Wardlaw Reid* (Peckham Rye), J. B. Richardson* (Dumfries), Wm. Rome* (London), Thomas Stordy (Cumberland Union Bank, Carlisle), H. M. Swindells* (Oxford), Wm. Tinline (Galashiels), Walter Wallace (Kirkcudbright), and Thomas Welsh* (Selkirk).[1]

[1] All those names marked with an asterisk were members of the original committee.

At the meeting referred to above there was a stated definition of the breed Standard made and a firm adoption of the Standard given at a meeting on the 5th September, 1876. Several amendments were made in 1877, 1892 and 1901, and the current breed Standard reads as follows:

HEAD AND SKULL

Head strongly made and large, not out of proportion to the dog's size, the muscles showing extraordinary development, more especially the maxillary. Skull broad between the ears, getting gradually less towards the eye, and measuring about the same from the inner corner of the eye to the back of the skull as it does from ear to ear. The forehead well domed. The head is covered with very soft silky hair, which should not be confined to a mere top-knot, and the lighter in colour and silkier it is the better. The cheeks, starting from the ears proportionately with the skull, have a gradual taper towards the muzzle, which is deep and strongly made, and measures about three inches in length, or in proportion to skull as three is to five. The muzzle is covered with hair of a little darker shade than the top-knot, and of the same texture as the feather of the forelegs. The top of the muzzle is generally bare for about an inch from the back part of the nose, the bareness coming to a point towards the eye, and being about one inch broad at the nose. The nose black.

EYES

Set wide apart, large, full, round but not protruding, bright, expressive of great determination, intelligence and dignity, set low and prominent in front of the head, colour a rich dark hazel.

EARS

Pendulous, set well back, wide apart and low on the skull, hanging close to the cheek, with a very slight projection at the base; broad at the junction of the head and tapering almost to a point, the fore part of the ear coming almost straight down from its junction with the head to the tip. They shall harmonise in colour with body colour. On a pepper dog they are covered with a soft straight dark hair (in some cases almost black). On a mustard dog,

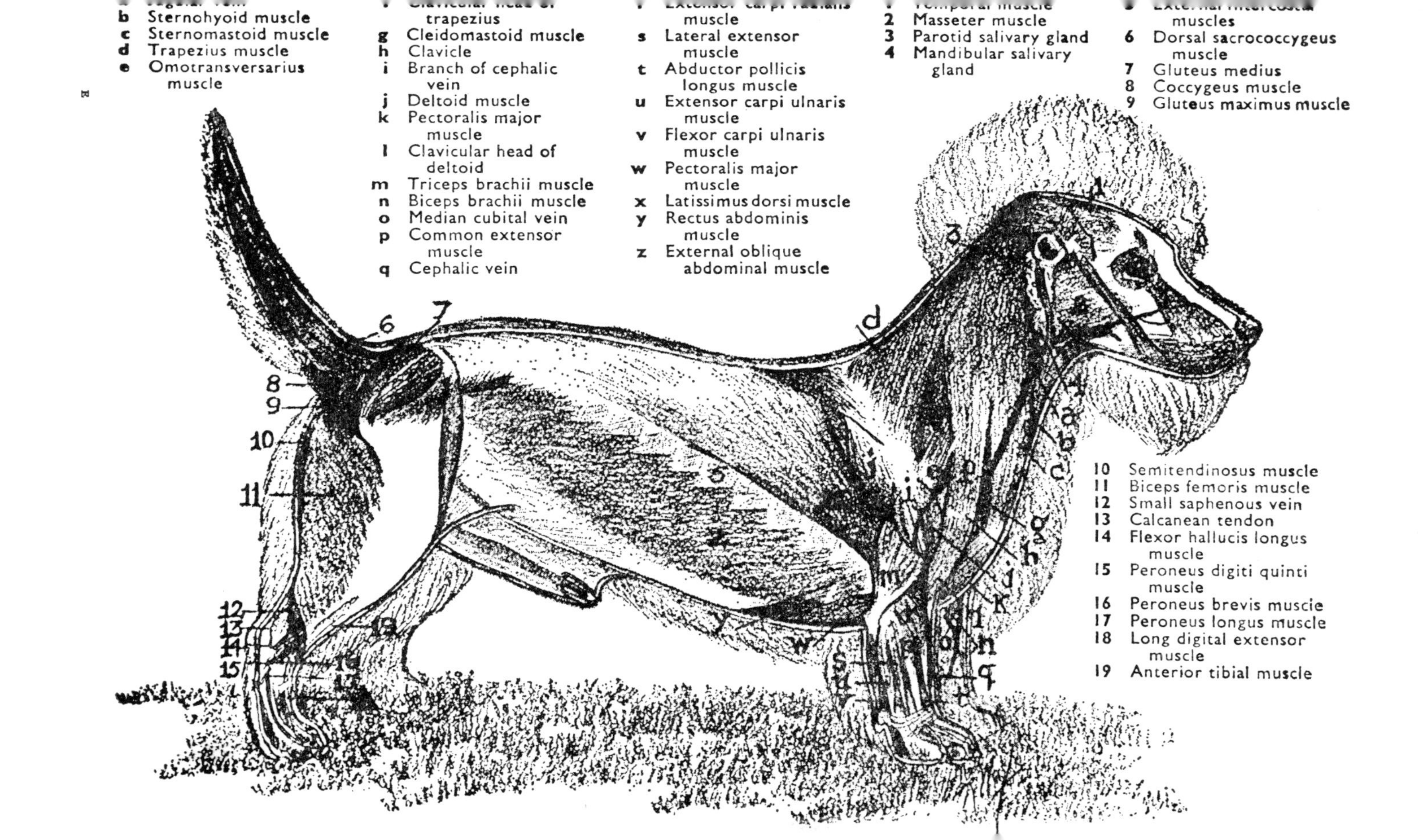

b Sternohyoid muscle
c Sternomastoid muscle
d Trapezius muscle
e Omotransversarius muscle
trapezius
g Cleidomastoid muscle
h Clavicle
i Branch of cephalic vein
j Deltoid muscle
k Pectoralis major muscle
l Clavicular head of deltoid
m Triceps brachii muscle
n Biceps brachii muscle
o Median cubital vein
p Common extensor muscle
q Cephalic vein
muscle
s Lateral extensor muscle
t Abductor pollicis longus muscle
u Extensor carpi ulnaris muscle
v Flexor carpi ulnaris muscle
w Pectoralis major muscle
x Latissimus dorsi muscle
y Rectus abdominis muscle
z External oblique abdominal muscle
2 Masseter muscle
3 Parotid salivary gland
4 Mandibular salivary gland
muscles
6 Dorsal sacrococcygeus muscle
7 Gluteus medius
8 Coccygeus muscle
9 Gluteus maximus muscle
10 Semitendinosus muscle
11 Biceps femoris muscle
12 Small saphenous vein
13 Calcanean tendon
14 Flexor hallucis longus muscle
15 Peroneus digiti quinti muscle
16 Peroneus brevis muscle
17 Peroneus longus muscle
18 Long digital extensor muscle
19 Anterior tibial muscle

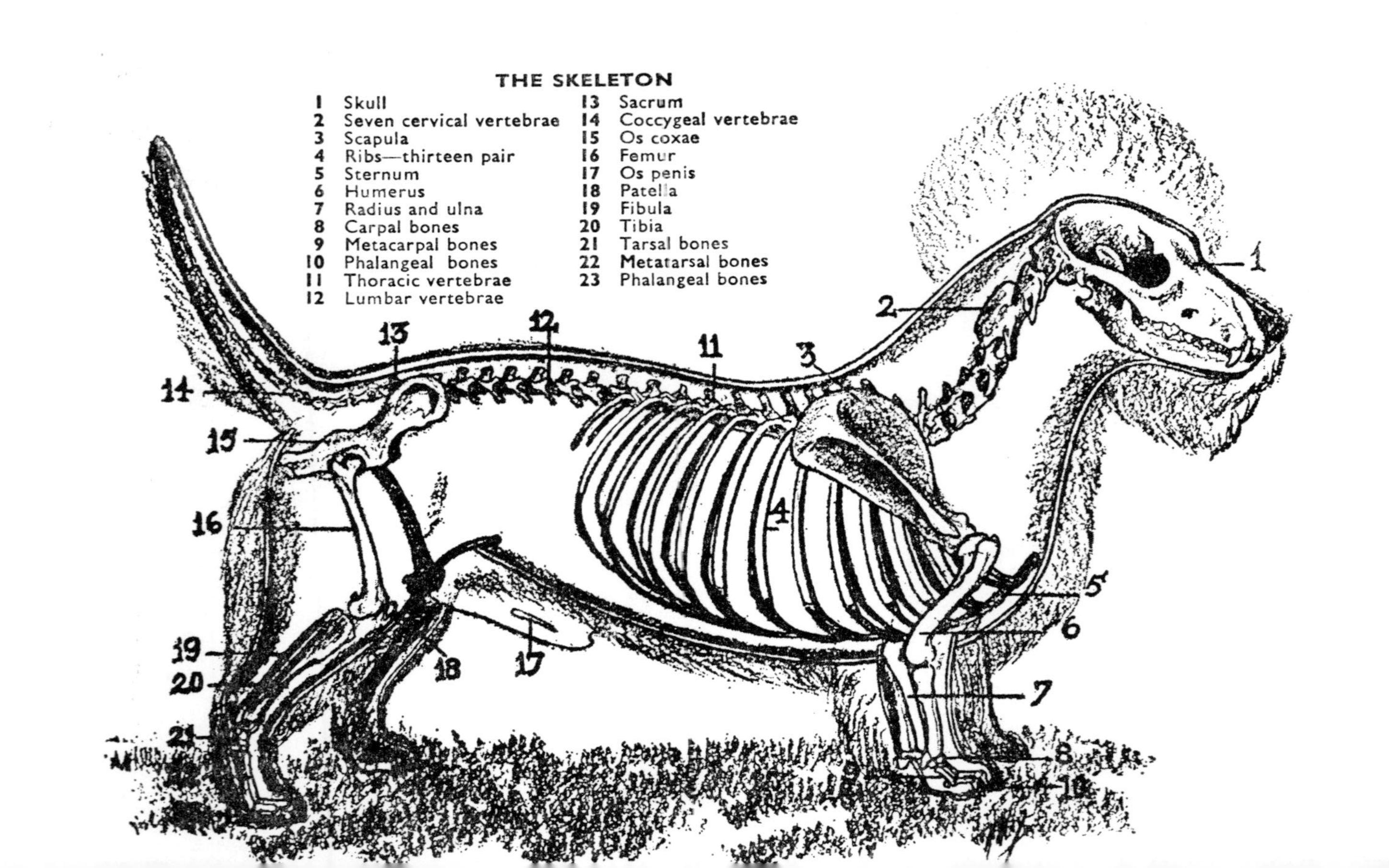
THE SKELETON
1 Skull
2 Seven cervical vertebrae
3 Scapula
4 Ribs—thirteen pair
5 Sternum
6 Humerus
7 Radius and ulna
8 Carpal bones
9 Metacarpal bones
10 Phalangeal bones
11 Thoracic vertebrae
12 Lumbar vertebrae
13 Sacrum
14 Coccygeal vertebrae
15 Os coxae
16 Femur
17 Os penis
18 Patella
19 Fibula
20 Tibia
21 Tarsal bones
22 Metatarsal bones
23 Phalangeal bones
1
2
3
4
5
6
7
8
10
11
12
13
14
15
16
17
18
19
20
21

the hair should be mustard in colour, a shade darker than the body but not black. All should have a thin feather of light hair starting about two inches from the tip, and of nearly the same colour and texture as the top-knot, which gives the ear the appearance of a distinct point. The animal is often one or two years old before the feather is shown. The cartilage and skin of the ear should not be thick, but very thin. Length of ear, from three to four inches.

Mouth

The inside of the mouth should be black or dark coloured. The teeth very strong, especially the canines, which are of extraordinary size for such a small dog. The canines fit well into each other, so as to give the greatest available holding and punishing power, and the teeth are level in front, the upper ones very slightly overlapping the under ones. Undershot or overshot mouths are equally objectionable.

Neck

Very muscular, well developed, and strong, showing great power of resistance, being well set into the shoulders.

Forequarters

The forelegs short, with immense muscular development and

A. Correct. Sound front

B. Unsound Front. Weak at Pasterns.

bone, set wide apart and chest coming well down between them. Bandy legs are objectionable. The hair on the forelegs of a pepper dog should be tan, varying according to the body colour from a rich tan to a pale fawn; of a mustard dog they are of a darker shade than its head, which is creamy white. In both colours there is a nice feather about two inches long, rather lighter in colour than the hair on the forepart of the leg.

Body

Long, strong and flexible; ribs well sprung and round, chest well developed and let well down between the forelegs; the back rather low at the shoulders having a slight downward curve and a corresponding arch over the loins, with a very slight gradual drop from top of loin to root of tail; both sides of backbone well supplied with muscle.

Hindquarters

The hind legs are a little longer than the fore and are set rather wide apart, but not spread out in an unnatural manner; the thighs are well developed, and the hair of the same colour and texture as on the forelegs, but having no feather or dew-claws.

Feet

Flat feet are objectionable. The whole claws should be dark, but the claws of all vary in shade according to the colour of the dog's body. The feet of a pepper dog should be tan, varying according to the body colour from a rich tan to a pale fawn; of a mustard dog they are a shade darker than its head. Hind feet should be much smaller than the forefeet.

Tail

Rather short, say from eight to ten inches, and covered on the upper side with wiry hair of a darker colour than that of the body, the hair on the under side being lighter in colour, and not so wiry, with a nice feather about two inches long, getting shorter as it nears the tip; rather thick at the root, getting thicker for about four inches, then tapering off to a point. It should not be twisted or curled in any way, but should come up with a curve like a scimitar, the tip, when excited, being in a perpendicular line with the root of the tail. It should neither be set too high nor too low. When not excited it is carried gaily, and a little above the level of the body.

A. Unsound Body. 'Swamp' or dipped Back just behind the shoulders.

B. Too straight Topline. Back too short.

C. Long-neck, insufficient development over loin.

D. Roach Back. Curve starts from just behind the shoulders.

E. Stern-high. Backline slopes up from behind shoulders to set-on of Tail.

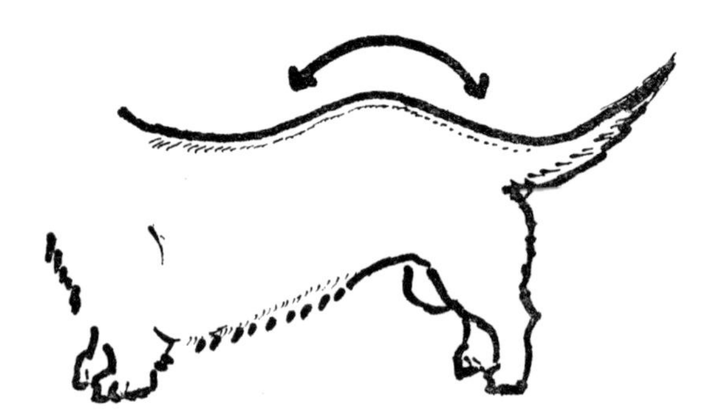

F. Over-rise of loin, with fall away at Croup.

G. Correct Outline

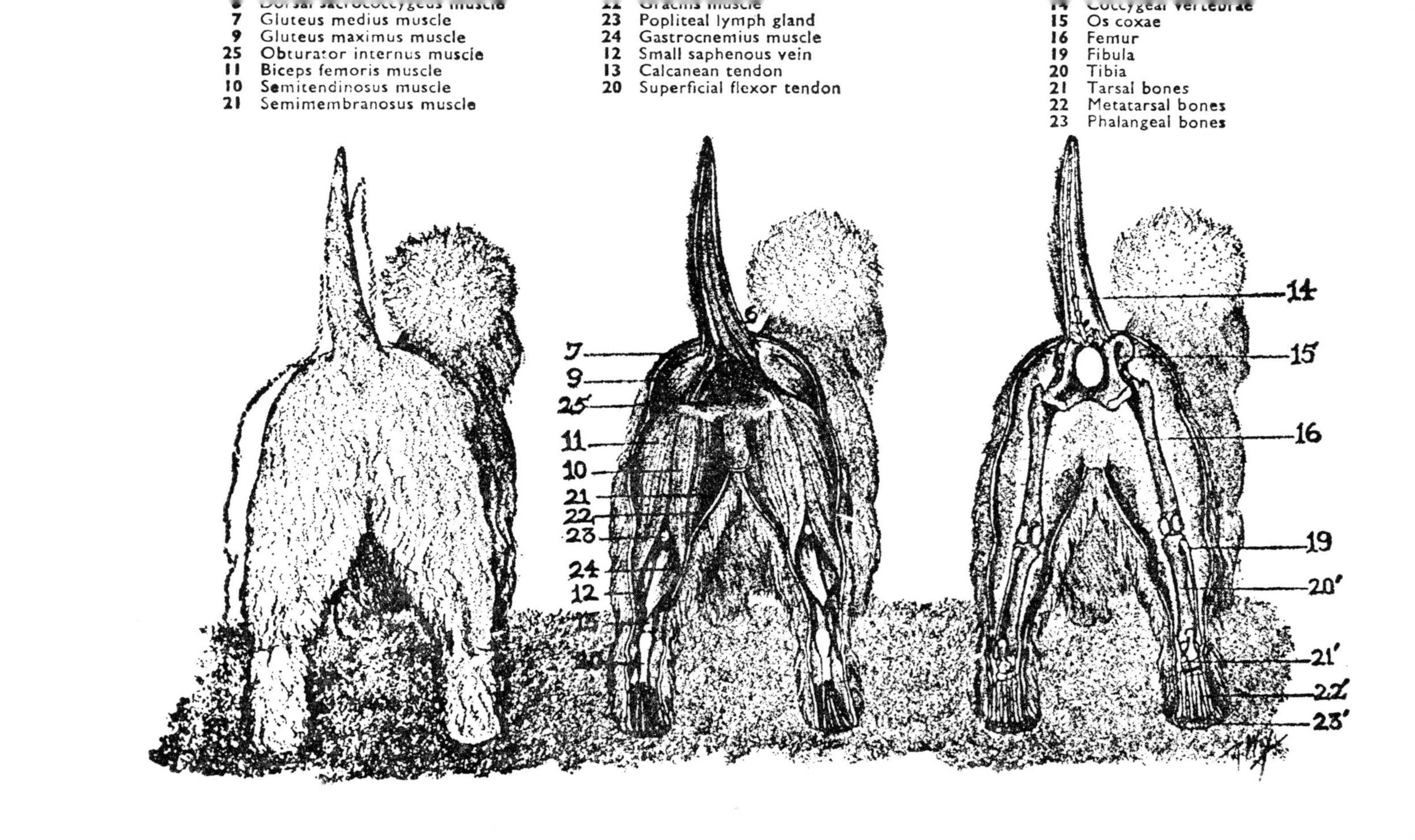
7 Gluteus medius muscle
9 Gluteus maximus muscle
25 Obturator internus muscle
11 Biceps femoris muscle
10 Semitendinosus muscle
21 Semimembranosus muscle
23 Popliteal lymph gland
24 Gastrocnemius muscle
12 Small saphenous vein
13 Calcanean tendon
20 Superficial flexor tendon
15 Os coxae
16 Femur
19 Fibula
20 Tibia
21 Tarsal bones
22 Metatarsal bones
23 Phalangeal bones
6
7
9
25
11
10
21
22
23
24
12
14
15
16
19
20'
21'
22'
23'

A. Cow Hocks. Points of Hocks turn in to each other. Back Feet turn out.

B. Correct Hindquarters

C. In-toed. Feet point in and Hocks turn out away from each other

Coat

The coat is a very important point. The hair should be about two inches long; that from the skull to root of tail a mixture of hardish and soft hair, which gives a sort of crisp feel to the hand. The hair should not be wiry; the coat is termed pily or pencilled. The hair on the under part of the body is lighter in colour and softer than that on top. The skin on the belly accords with the colour of the dog.

Colour

The colour is pepper or mustard. The pepper ranges from a dark bluish black to a light silvery grey, the intermediate shades being preferred, the body colour coming well down the shoulder and hips, gradually merging into the leg colour. The mustards vary from a reddish brown to a pale fawn, the head being creamy white, the legs and feet of a darker shade than the head. The claws are dark as in other colours. (Nearly all Dandie Dinmont Terriers have some white on the chest, and some have white claws.) White feet are objectionable.

Weight and Size

The height should be from eight to eleven inches at the top of the shoulder. Length from top of shoulder to root of tail should not be more than twice the dog's height, but, preferably, one or two

c Sternomastoid muscle
d Trapezius muscle
e Omotransversarius muscle
f Clavicular head of trapezius
g Cleido-mastoid muscle

i Branch of cephalic vein
j Deltoid muscle
k Pectoralis major muscle
l Clavicular head of deltoid
m Triceps brachii muscle
n Biceps brachii muscle

p Common extensor muscle
q Cephalic vein
r Extensor carpi-radialis
s Lateral extensor muscle
t Abductor pollicis longus
u Accessory cephalic vein

2 Cervical vertebrae
3 Scapula
4 Ribs
5 Sternum
6 Humerus
7 Radius and ulna
8 Carpal bones
9 Metacarpal bones
10 Phalangeal bones

inches less. The ideal weight as near eighteen pounds as possible. These weights are for dogs in good working order.

Reproduced by kind permission of The Kennel Club

SCALE OF POINTS

The latest Standard issued by the Kennel Club does not include a Scale of Points as did the original issues of the Standards of the breeds. It is apparent that the use of such an arbitrary system of grading is not generally approved by this body. However, I give the original Scale of Points showing their relative values in the Standard here for those who are interested.

Head	10
Eyes	10
Ears	10
Neck	5
Body	20
Tail	5
Legs and Feet	10
Coat	15
Colour	5
Weight and Size	5
General Appearance	5
Total	100

COMMENTS ON THE STANDARD

The foregoing Standard, originally drafted by the Dandie Dinmont Terrier Club, although exhaustive in its way, like the Standards of other breeds, can be in itself little more than a guide as to what is considered to constitute the perfect Dandie Dinmont Terrier. Such matters, and vital matters they are, as character, temperament, movement, expression, style, type and so on cannot adequately be assessed from the written word; a dog may be virtually perfect in that he fits the description of the Standard, but because he lacks one or more of the characteristics just referred to he may not in effect be a Dandie of the kind required. This may seem a paradox, but if the reader considers the various points of the Standard one by one, he will realise that whereas each and every section of the specimen under review may individually conform to Standard requirements, these sections when put together to make the total dog may well not please because the linking of the parts is imperfect either for lack of true physical soundness or from some defect in the animal's breeding. The deficiency may show itself in expression, or in character, or breed type (at best an almost indefinable quality), or in some inherent nervousness which will detract at once from a pleasurable appreciation of the dog being judged.

The following additional remarks on the Standard should be read in conjunction with the official description and may serve to amplify the various sections.

Head and Skull

It is stated that the forehead should be well domed. Any sign of 'peaking' at the back of the skull in the fashion of a Bloodhound is undesirable. The Dandie's head must be large and strong, but it should be remembered that the large head should not be a heavy, dull and cumbrous head, but typical enough of his Terrier ancestry. The casual observer is inclined to accept the Dandie's head as larger than it is in fact due to the added visual size accorded to it by the liberal hirsute head adornment known as the top-knot.

Eyes

The eyes are probably best described as being dark and 'melting', capable however of flashing fire when aroused. The colour should be dark hazel, so dark in fact as for the iris to appear black at a short distance. This, of course, should apply to peppers and mustards alike, although a slightly lighter eye is tolerated in the latter. Further, correct placement of the eyes is important too. If the large, full, dark, luminous eyes are set wide apart, are spectacled and set low in the skull, the expression will deepen to the desired effect. So far as expression itself is concerned, the quotation of David Baillie when asked to describe the correct Dandie expression, is right to the point. He said: 'He should look at ye, ma'am, as much as to say, I hae forgot mair than ever ye kent.'

Ears

These are required to be pendulous and are reasonably large in relation to the size of the breed. However, they should not be like those of the Hound as indeed they may appear to be if too large. On the other hand too small ears seldom if ever hang properly. In some exhibits the fault lies with the ears being too broad towards the tips at which point they should in fact narrow rather sharply. The front edge of the ears should run in a straight line, not a curve, from head to lower tip, the tapering being achieved by the line of the back part of the ears. The correct filbert-shaped ears should not hang in true perpendicular, but should incline *slightly* forward towards the eye, and should be set on the head fairly low and lie in close to the cheek.

Mouth

Much controversy has raged on the subject of undershot and overshot mouths. However, it is clear beyond all doubt in the minds of experienced breeders of the Dandie Dinmont that *badly* undershot and overshot mouths are to be avoided in the planning of their matings. Contrary to some opinions, I believe that the badly overshot mouth is the prime offender of the two faults, although even this when *slight* is superior to the 'flush' mouth (upper and lower incisors meeting tip to tip) which has nothing to redeem it. The 'pig-jaw' (or 'swine-mouth' as it is sometimes called) can be effective in tearing, but it lacks full strength and so often the jaw formation of this fault is accompanied by a mean skull and snipy muzzle, both physical weaknesses. The badly undershot jaw for its part can bruise in its hold, but it lacks the clean scissor or shearing action of the true level Terrier mouth. Likewise dogs with badly undershot mouths so often possess an untypical coarseness of visage and the whole contour of the head is spoilt. Both faults are serious and have little or nothing to justify their acceptance, although I have found in work that the undershot variety is relatively less unserviceable than the overshot dog which is useless —anyway both kinds should be rejected. With dogs only slightly affected by the faults some forbearance may be observed, although it is a case of the thin edge of the wedge. In the show ring, at least, there is no reason at all why an excellent specimen affected *slightly* with either of these faults should not be allowed to win cards. However, all other points being equal, the level-mouthed dog must take priority to him in a judge's placings.

The Dandie's large strong teeth are proverbial. The jaw muscles which actuate the lower jaw allow a powerful bite and he can mete out great punishment to his quarry. The muzzle must be deep and strongly made to justify this stout machinery, and although a fine muzzle may be able to work reasonably well, more often than not it is associated with inferior muscular development in the maxillaries.

Feet and Forequarters

Working ability in the Dandie must always have the conscientious breeder's leading consideration. Well-made, comparatively straight forelegs with strong bone, clean, well-laid-back shoulders and firmly knit feet are essential in an earth dog to allow him maximum activity and endurance. Thin, flat feet are bad faults in the Dandie as with any Terrier breed. A *slight* outward cant of the feet can be accepted providing the toes are well arched with strong claws.

Body

The true Dandie topline is a prized and beautiful characteristic of the breed, and has to be preserved. At times many misconceptions have existed as to the true line of the body when viewed in profile, not the least among them being the incorrect use of the word 'roach' in describing it.

Attention to the Standard will show that the back should be rather low at the shoulders, having a slight *downward* curve and a corresponding arch over the loins. This description infers then that the corresponding arch over the loins is also slight, and no such back can be fairly described as 'roach'. The true 'roach' back, as typified by the Borzoi, starts its rise immediately behind the withers, and continues in an unbroken convex line down to the stern. No correctly made Dandie should have such a topline; if he has, then he may well be unsound in front with rickety fore-legs.

An exaggerated dip behind the shoulders and a correspondingly broad arch over the loins is also incorrect. Such dogs usually fail in their set-on of tail. Alternatively, a Dandie may be too long in his hind legs, making his topline run straight up from withers to tail. Such specimens are usually described as 'stern-high' and the fault is a bad one, although possibly not so distasteful to the breed lover as a level, straight topline.

It will be admitted that some Dandies have an exaggerated development of the loin, shown in a hump-like curve, and although these may not necessarily be unsound specimens they show an exaggeration of a breed asset, and are therefore faulty. Some may consider such dogs useful at stud to remedy the menace of the level back and indeed many would appear to have done this, but this is really a fallacy for it would mean virtually mating one fault to another fault.

The body should be long and flexible and shaped like that of a weasel. Dependent upon correct body shape and mechanics is the true Dandie movement, which is quite distinct from that of other Terrier breeds. The correct body construction demands a long broad shoulder blade (scapula), well laid back at roughly right-angles to the upper arm (humerus) allowing the deep Dandie chest to be bounded on both sides by the forelegs. The Dandie's body is long and arched, and it is necessary for the lumbar region to be well muscled and developed in order to induce power for propulsion. On a long flexible body such as the Dandie's supported as it is on quite short legs, all muscles must be strongly developed and supple. The main back muscles control and co-ordinate the action and pace of the forequarters and hindquarters, and if the mechanics are sound, then the movement will be balanced and sound also.

Tail

Although the Dandie carries his tail in perhaps a Hound style, he should not have a Hound's tail; this should be essentially Terrier in character. An unpleasant effect is given when the tail is too long, and in fact a short, gaily carried scimitar-like tail is part of the true Dandie make-up. The whole effect of correct tail carriage can be lost, however, by poor set-on, which should be neither too low nor too high on the back. The hair on the tail is generally a little harder to the touch than that on the body which it matches in colour. The underside should be tan.

Hindquarters

The hindquarters must have a well-angled conformation. Incorrect angulation produces the long flat thighs which are objectionable, not only because they detract from soundness but because they render movement untypical in the Dandie. As I have said, the main back muscles co-ordinate the front and hind movement via the body. If the hindquarters are faulty or possess any weakness, they will not work in correct rhythm with the forequarters, and vice versa, and so an added burden is put on to the sound end of the dog, whereupon movement must fail. The powerful back muscles cause the forward pelvic slide that creates the 'roll' typical of the Dandie. This unique movement is emphasised by the shape of the Dandie's long body in comparison with his short legs.

Soundness and the fixing of desirable points in the breed has generally improved especially over the last two decades, but many breeders still need to show a little more interest in dogs other than their own. Mediocre bitches should not be preserved and used for breeding, but should be scrapped and their places filled with more desirable specimens who can contribute a greater worth to the breed.

A number of the more conscientious breeders have for long been aware of the dangers associated with the improvement of legs and feet, which in certain cases has inclined the Dandie's back to a displeasing shortness after the Terrier mode. The natural attractive Dandie topline is a prized heritage and it must never be straightened or modified in association with shallow briskets.

Good legs and feet may be more easily obtained in a shorter, lighter specimen, in fact care must ever be taken to ensure that improvement in some features does not work to the disadvantage of others. The typical Dandie has to have good quarters and feet if he is to move with the air of independence and dignity expected of his breed. Many such improvements have been effected due to the work of careful breeders, and it is incumbent on the fancy in general to implement their successes with perhaps a broader appreciation of the breeder's art.

Coat

The Dandie is a rough-coated Terrier, but not hard or broken-haired as were some of his original ancestors. A good double coat is required, single-coated specimens being at a severe disadvantage in the show ring. The coat should not be too profuse, and that on the upper body and neck should be preferably of a texture described in the original Club edict as 'a mixture of about two-thirds rather hard (but not wiry) hair, with one-third soft, linty (not silky) hair, which gives a sort of crisp feeling to the hand', in brief a 'pily' coat.

The coat should lie in 'pencils' down the back rather than be 'shed'. This is due to the undercoat being in the main of soft hair, through which the longer and harder hair comes in firm tufts. This forms a coat protective to wet and cold, and quick-drying when damp or wet. Occasionally, one notes specimens with coats of short, hard hair, without the beautifying effect of the soft hair undercoat. Such animals will invariably be deficient or even lack top-knot, and this is completely alien to the breed. Thus, it will be seen how important it is to consider a correctly mixed coat in parents and ancestors when planning a mating.

The Dandie's top-knot, which has been referred to as his 'crowning glory', is dependent in the main on true coat texture. If the coat is wrongly composed then the quality of the top-knot must inevitably suffer. It will be agreed that there are Dandie owners who care very little for such ornamentation, preferring their dogs to be good utility specimens rather than pretty ones. That may be sound opinion, but a dog can be useful and made beautiful too with judicious applications to his natural assets.

In the Dandie, nothing could be more attractive than a lustrous, well-furnished top-knot, silvery-white in the pepper and creamy-white in the mustard. This silky head-covering in its perfect form, covers the whole of the top of the head, across between the ears, then from above the eyes, where the forelock falls softly and gently forward over the stop, to the back of the skull or occiput where it ends sharply and stylishly. The top-knot should stand up in slightly twirled locks or 'pencils' pointing rather forwards in front.

Colour

It is said that no good dog can be a bad colour, and this again is entirely a working sentiment. In the show ring, fanciers demand certain exactnesses in colour and markings, and today the traditional colours of pepper and mustard are kept and bred distinct in the individual specimens. Body colour should extend always well down on the shoulders and thighs, and the tan should be pale or fawn, not mahogany red.

Weight and Size

These are also factors which have caused controversy in the past, and indeed do so still. It is certain that the Dandie of yester-year was a smaller dog than he is today. It is stated that James Davidson preferred them not heavier than 16 lb. Francis Somner wrote that his average was 15 lb, and 'for every lb less he valued them £1 more'! Drygrange Charlie, the sire of Shem, was only 12 lb and, Nettle, the bitch acquired by Mr. Somner from Hindlee, weighed only 11 lb. There were certain so-called Dandies in the period who went 24 lb or more, but these were most likely impure kinds such as were bred at Arks and Gateshaw and districts, and history tells us that they were from the original peppers and mustards crossed with a large rough-haired 'Otter Terrier' and as such could not claim to be true Dandies. Personally, I prefer the more active, smaller kind of Dandie Dinmont Terrier.

A heavy dog may be all right for the introduction of stamina, bone and substance when and where it is needed in a breeding programme, but a true Dandie has to be a busy, smart Terrier, eager in mind and flexible in his body. He has to be of a size and weight to cope with the fox in its earth. The average weight of a fox is 10 lb or 11 lb, though some weigh more, depending, of course, upon their location, and in practice generally any dog required to go to ground after him must needs be of approximate weight or very slightly heavier for advantage in combat. A dog of say 20 lb could not so easily go to ground and although we are today largely concerned with the breeding of show stock, the original uses of the Dandie must never be forgotten.

The Dandie Dinmont Terrier Club, when it drew up the breed Standard, insisted that the *maximum* weight of a dog should be 24 lb and advised 18 lb as to the weight to be bred for. A dog of this weight can have all the abilities of a true Dandie in practical work, and yet be well clear of any suggestion of weediness.

Anyone in doubt as to what constitutes correct coat in the

Dandie (and judging by breed comment, both vocal and written, some fanciers do not know what to breed for in coat) should read pages 104–9 in Cook's monograph. Here can be found not only a detailed description of correct coat, but much to learn from the author's supplementary remarks.

John Valance writing in *The Scottish Fancier and Rural Gazette* in 1887 contributes to an argument about Dandie Dinmont weight which was raging in the press at that time. Referring to Robert Fortune, molecatcher on Lord Lauderdale's estate, who never had less than four or five at his heels, the smallest of these being a little over 18 lb. He says the rest were between 20–24 lbs and the time he wrote about was 1847. Others of the era—Mr. Purvis, farmer of Leaderfoot, Matthew and John Kennedy, tinkers and mugger-muggers of Selkirk—all had Dandies which were around the 24 lb-mark. Mr. Simpson of Threepwood and his brother of Blainsley kept a kennel of Dandies nearer the weight of 30lb. Mr. Luig of Uddingstone, a great fox-hunting squire, kept a 'whole swarm' of about fifty Dandies and they too were all of substantial weight. He comments on the stock of Mr. Nicol Milne of Faldonside, mentioned earlier in this book. These, Mr. Valance says, were not much less than 28 lb, one named Tinker in particular being a big dog. He saw Mr. James Scott's ('Newstead') in Galashiels one day with three saddle-backed Dandies, all between 20–25 lb. Of course, these were the days when no one minded much a cross with an Otterhound if the result was to make a dog which was improved on its parents in usefulness. Every breed, as far as I am aware, has gone through a period in its history when weight has been the subject of much controversy. It was all part of their 'growing pains'. In the Dandie world the matter has been reasonably well settled and they like a show dog to weigh about 18 lb. It is essential to keep to the exhibition requirement quite rigidly and let those who want a Dandie for other than show work adapt it for their particular needs and maintain it and breed it in its own sphere.

TRUE CHARACTER AND TEMPERAMENT

Much has been written in the past of these essential ingredients of the Dandie Dinmont Terrier. They are subjects which concern me greatly, not only in this grand little breed, but in other Terriers where correct temperament and character stand in danger of dilution, even disappearance. Unfortunately, in certain strains, the cherished characteristic of hard-bitten gameness has gone, probably for good. This is because those who have owned the dogs have cared nothing for it, and let it slip through their fingers in favour of fanciers' points many of which are useless to the breed.

The original Dandie Dinmont was a plucky, fearless sort of dog, indifferent to hardship and bad weathers, and ready to tackle animals far larger and stronger than himself. As a killer of vermin he was without peer, and seldom would you hear him cry out if hurt.

In Sir Walter Scott's *Guy Mannering* we have a pointer to the Dandie's character in the lines: '. . . I have six terriers at hame, forbye two couple of slowhunds, five grews, and a wheen other dogs. There's auld Pepper and auld Mustard, and young Pepper and young Mustard, and little Pepper and little Mustard—I had them a' regularly entered, first wi' rottens—then wi' stots or weasels—and then wi' the tods and brocks—and now they fear naething that ever cam' wi' a hairy skin on't.' From these words we can savour in full the spirit of the Dandie of nearly 150 years ago.

We should heed the advice of Scott's own line which reads: 'Beast or body, education should aye be minded', and indeed we should mind in full the education of our dogs, to preserve the true Dandie spirit, by working them as much as we are able, or to consider seriously the use at stud of dogs known to possess the desired character. If we ignore gameness and general toughness, then as has been proved in the histories of other once courageous breeds, the Dandie will fade into a gloomy obscurity.

Many Dandie Dinmonts as puppies are prone to shyness. This to the dismay of many owners who at once will claim inbreeding and nervousness in the strain. In such cases, patience is needed, for many finely bred dogs are rather inclined this way in early puppyhood—it is the ingredient of the thoroughbred which so often produces a keen sensitivity. Many Dandies do not show their true colours in correct temperament and character until they are at least eighteen months old, by which time the average dog has proved that he has the very essence of what is required in a game

Terrier. Many of these dogs are slow to rouse, and in fact may even need provoking before setting to, but once their blood is up, they become veritable demons in attack. As young puppies they may well nurse an insult for quite a long time, and when the opportunity presents itself later will seek a full revenge. They possess a somewhat excitable nature, and for such small dogs are quite pugnacious. Yet in work they are very cool and thorough, doing their job with the minimum of fuss. This characteristic makes them invaluable in the field.

For those who are interested in the working Dandie, it is as well not to enter your Terrier until he is at least one year old, although some puppies show a useful tendency to work before this age. In such cases intelligent discrimination must be used, for a young puppy can be spoilt if he gets hurt too soon in life.

THE WORKING DANDIE

The Dandie Dinmont Terrier was used originally as a working Terrier for going to ground to fox, badger and otter, quite apart from being employed generally around the farm and fields as a vermin exterminator. At all these things he excelled and because of it a Dandie or two in sporting homes was at one time quite commonplace. However, today with urban encroachment on our countryside the larger wild mammals are becoming scarce and it is not particularly easy for the countryman, let alone the town-dweller to find terrain where game is readily available. Consequently, good, game working Dandies are fewer and anyone with one or more of these worthy canines has treasure indeed.

If you are fortunate enough to be near a rural region where game can be successfully sought, you can test your Dandie's mettle without delay, but he must have some training first. Raw dogs at this game are a nuisance and interfere with the proper running of the sport. If you are keen to work the dog it is as well to get him interested while still fairly young and six months is not a bad age at which to start, although some prefer the puppy rather older. A lot depends on the puppy's development and mentality. In any case, it is best to begin with a rat and let him kill it. This will whet his appetite and prepare him for larger and more formidable game, arousing in him instincts which are his natural heritage.

Temperament, although subdued in many modern breeds is never really lost and the average Dandie today, unless he has been ruined by his owner's lap-dog treatment is quite likely to surprise you by his readiness to tackle and deal effectively with vermin. A good working weight for a mature Dandie is between 12 and 16 lbs but if you contemplate digging for badger, then you will need a dog topping 20 lb. He should be particularly strong in jaw, neck, back and shoulders. A dog with bossy shoulders and out at elbow is useless as he will probably get stuck in the hole and make a nuisance of himself as you will have to dig him out and waste time. He will need a deep, well-rounded rib cage and possess plenty of lung and heart room in his skeletal make-up. To be low to ground is best, although in a working dog this is not essential. A dog lies on his side and scratches and scrambles his way into a hole—he does not just lower his head and dash in! Make sure if a working Dandie is your aim to buy him from a reliable working strain from pedigree breeding which can be traced back with working dogs for years.

RATTING

This is a 'sport' despised by many who have graduated their dogs to bolt the fox and work to badger. Nevertheless, it starts off a young dog well for his hunting career and fulfils a useful function to the community. The first thing is to ensure that your puppy has been properly vaccinated against leptospiral infection which is passed on by rats. This is important. Some dogs can kill their first rat when about six months of age. It is not a good thing to let him try earlier than this as a bad bite can prove a set-back from which he might take a long time to readjust from. The best way to train a dog to anything is to use an older and experienced dog as a tutor. The youngster will watch his mentor's every move and speedily emulate them. This will achieve much better results than any human training at this work. The rats should be obtained from a local rat-catcher and caged. Let the youngster see the quarry in the cage; he will become excited and pulling at his leash appear ready to go. Release one rat in a field with short grass and let the older dog who is teaching kill it. This he will do immediately and will be watched intently by the youngster, who when his turn comes will rush at the released rat. Some puppies kill without fuss, others are unsure what to do. They will merely chase the quarry, run round it barking without taking hold. Do *not* encourage the slow learner. If he has the right stuff in him and is bred right, he will soon pick up instinctively what he is supposed to do. If you have several puppies to train in this way, put them to rat one at a time. If you let a brace work together they will probably start fighting, lose the rat and learn nothing.

The next stage is to train your puppy to go to earth. A hole should be dug at an angle about eighteen inches deep and a rat placed at the bottom. The rodent will not scuttle out as it will know the dog is near by above ground. Then let the Dandie go and he will mark the rat to ground, dig it out and dispatch it. From that moment holes in the ground will interest him and imbue him with the idea that they are good for finding vermin.

FOX

Once reasonably proficient at killing rats, the puppy or young dog can now be trained to fox. This is a rather different story for a dog can get a nasty bite from the fox and if he is entered too young you may well spoil him. If your dog seems well grown, strong and ready and he should be really at least a year old he can be tried, but carefully. Fox is his natural quarry and providing he is not too brash and impetuous he will probably make a good job of his first lesson. This should take the form of a 'walk' behind a local meet. Never intrude on such an event without first gaining permission from the huntsman. Try and bring your Dandie (he will be on a lead, of course!) near enough to what is going on so that he can hear the hunt terrier baying the fox below ground. If possible, let your dog see the fox killed and again, if possible, try and secure a piece of the animal for him to acquaint him with its taste and scent. If you are fortunate enough to see an opportunity and get permission to enter your dog once the fox has been dug down to, grab the chance with both hands! Do not pressure your dog with either words or action—just take him to the scene of action, release him and he should go straight in quite naturally. If he comes in too close and starts mixing it with the fox best pull him out in case he gets badly punished, for this will do him no good.

Make a fuss of him for trying, however, and if the hunt terriers accept him, he might be able to join them and be in at the kill. It should be remembered that some Dandies are very slow to enter in this way. This need occasion no disappointment and even if you have to wait until the dog is eighteen months or more before he proves himself it will be worth it; slow-maturers often turn out best. Cub-hunting is another good way of introducing a youngster to fox. Most of the packs are occupied with this in early autumn and the meets make a youngster's education to fox interesting and effective. You may get a chance to enter your dog, subject to permission, and at the same time get useful opinions as to your dog's potential from some of the old hands almost certain to be present.

BADGER

Brock, as the badger is sometimes known is a nocturnal creature. He is a much-maligned animal who is accused at times of carnivorous activities with farmstock of which he is usually innocent. His numbers in this country are getting less, but a few remain still in their age-old setts. He is a formidable adversary and not one that any dog should come to grips with. The clever Terrier keeps just short of his fierce and mutilating bite. Only an idiot dog goes in and lays hold of a badger. I have known the Staffordshire Bull Terrier work to badger and come off second-best. Some have come out of the sett with half a face—one famous Stafford called Fearless Joe died from badger bite, so you can tell this mammal is more than a match for a Dandie. If ever you hear a Dandie has killed a badger check first if the latter was sick, exhausted or had been man-handled. No healthy badger in good fettle and of mature age is ever likely to have been killed by a Terrier breed. Nevertheless, a good Dandie-to-be must go to ground against the badger and stick with his quarry for a proper working period. The dog should be hard and cruel in his work and determined to the last in spite of the opposition. Some people prefer to hunt the badger at night when he is abroad. He invariably has to be dug to and it is not much use doing this unless there is a full moon. The usual procedure is to loose *one* dog down a likely looking hole in the sett. Other dogs should be tied up fast. If the dog comes into contact with Brock he will give voice—one that does not is quite useless, of course. Those above ground will then need to listen intently in order to locate the pair, and providing the barking goes on for a time, suggesting they are settled in one place they can be dug for. Some of the other exit holes of the labyrinth which makes up a typical badger sett should be stopped up with earth and branches. It is probably best to start digging at the mouth of the hole into which the Terrier was entered and follow it through from there. The badger will if he can try to gain a secure position in the main earth, well away from a blind tunnel or cul-de-sac where he will be cornered. If the Terrier comes out for a breather or because he has been bitten, another dog should be slipped in at once to keep him at bay, or you will lose the quarry. The usual procedure with the badger when captured is to 'bag' him and take him some fifteen or more miles away and release him in new surroundings. Bagging Brock though, is a job for the expert, and not for the newcomer to the game to try. This is usually done when the badger has been dug to and is clearly visible. The diggers will by now have departed from the scene—with alacrity no doubt and a good heavy Terrier should be able to draw Brock out for some stalwart to grab his tail, lift him with a shake and deposit him the bag held ready by the helpers. You will see that everyone involved with these final activities is well protected with strong high boots, for Brock is never averse to delivering a few never-to-be-forgotten bites on legs and feet if he is forced to charge through them! From all this you will observe that the sport is somewhat dangerous and certainly no game for an inexperienced dog.

OTTER

This is a sporting mammal, but hunting him is seldom engaged in today—at least not south of the borderlands. Here at one time it was extremely popular, the powerful Otterhound being employed in conjunction with Dandies and/or other suitable Terrier breeds, including Airedales. The otter is a hard and fast biter and, being a great swimmer, is capable of dragging down under water a Terrier of at least his own weight. The otter-hunting season is from April to October, the usual method being to draw upstream, although this is varied according to experience. Long ago they used to hunt the otter with a sort of trident and with nets, but although a steel-tipped lance is still used by some for probing under roots and in rushes where he might have taken refuge, today's sport is a cleaner one. The main thing is to locate the otter in his holt which is usually built under tree roots or boulders by the side of rivers, streams and mill pools. When found, and the Otterhound often does this—a Terrier is put in to cause the occupant to bolt. He usually goes up-river where he can find plenty of cover formed by rocks or bank projections. The animal often travels for quite long distances under water, the only indication as to its passage and progress being a 'chain' ripple formed on the surface of the water. It is not unusual for dogs to over-swim an otter and have to cast back, often losing him. It is important therefore to draw with care keeping an eye on both banks and to stop the hounds or dogs pushing forward too quickly. Every hole, projection, pipe or twisting root is a likely refuge for the quarry who possesses a good deal of cunning. He will endeavour to get into a deep, slow-running pool where he will have considerable advantage over the dogs. To prevent this, the hunters must try to pen him into a section of the water where he can be dealt with. The otter will then 'lie low' somewhere in the reeds giving no indication of his presence but if the hunt is a determined one he will soon be refound. This is why it is important to have at least an experienced dog or two in the pack. These knowing the otter's ways will persist at him whereas younger, inexperienced dogs get bored and give up the chase. The kill needs to be closely supervised if the dogs are to be saved damage for a cornered otter can inflict savage wounds.

In all these sports the Dandie Dinmont Terrier has for generations played an active and useful part. He is well adapted structurally and physically to participate with effect. The true temperament of his breed must never be lost and this is why show dogs should be introduced to the hunt of small game. Even stoat and rabbits can keep his blood coursing well if he is allowed to hunt them properly—although let it be said that the latter little animal is not a popular quarry with some huntsmen. They believe that a dog encouraged to hunt rabbit above ground may well not know when to relax his interest when entered to larger adversaries underground. Too often it seems have the hunt spent valuable time digging to a Terrier supposedly working to fox or badger only to find him lying-up to a petrified rabbit!

An example of the Dandie's propensities with rabbit in this respect is afforded by 'Stonehenge' (J. H. Walsh) once editor of *The Field* in his *The Dog, In Health and Disease*, 1879. He says while living in Worcestershire he owned in 1865 a dog called Rhoderick Dhu, given him by the Reverend J. C. Macdona. When this dog got scent of rabbit he became completely unmanageable and whether in covert or hedgerow he would persevere until actually restrained by force. Also, once the dog got into a wood it became hopeless to try and secure him until he was forced by hunger or sheer fatigue to desist; even punishment had no effect upon him. The dog was finally lost on Wimbledon Common where he got on to a rabbit scent and worked it out in the scrub. He did not lack either in his urge against fox. Walsh relates that on one occasion he killed five cubs in about as many minutes. His opinion was that however 'varmint' this temperament may be considered in a working dog it becomes a bore and a nuisance and for real work such a dog as this is useless.

The following snatch of 'home-spun' verse is of interest if only to serve the reader with the atmosphere of an old-time otter hunt.

It was written in 1905 to a well-known figure among Dandie pioneers—Archie Steel of Kelso by one who signed himself just 'J.M.'.

THE OTTER HUNT

In Kelso town there dwells a chiel
   An' that's ma auld friend, Archie Steel,
He's kenned, for miles the country roon,
   And by every one in Kelso Toon.
There's nane a Dandie Dinmont better knows
   For he is often judging at the shows,
And when he shows his Dandie dugs
   He aye comes hame wi' medals, cups or jugs
And its very seldom he is licket
   When competing for the special ticket.
And at walking matches, or otter hunt,
   You will always find him at the front.

Last year he was hunting up the Jed
  That day Lord Mole, the company led
And gave his head an awful thump
  Against a rotten auld tree stump.
That on his feet he could not stand
  But Archie he was close at hand
Took out his watch and fand his pulse,
  Quoth he: 'My Lord you're nane the worse
See: Here's some medicine I keep handy
  Just you take a tasting o' this brandy,
Do not be feart to take a guid and canty pull
  It soon will mend your auld crackit skull.
But leave a wee bit drappie for masel
  For faith it was ower the heid, I lately fell
I came doon with an awful whack
  When crossing at the auld cauld back,
So here's t'ye my Lord, now let's on the trail
An soon will have the otter by the tail.'
Then up the Teviotside they go
  With a wild whoop and a tally-ho
When a paling fence they tried to loup
  And they came dump down on their cloup,
Then at their hips they began to claw
  And curse the thing that made them fa',
But scarcely had they got on their pins
  And limping with their scarted shins,
When there they spied the otter's snoot
  At an auld tree root was keaking oot
But a terrier they soon had in the holt,
  That made the quarry his lair to bolt,
And into Nisbet dam it went splash
  But Rover at it made a dash,
Then with a loud whoop and blast of horn
  The poor beastie into shreds was torn.
The sport is now finished for the day
  And hameward now are on their way
When they thought a nip would wet their throttle
  But deil a drap was in their bottle.
When Archie goes hunting up the Tweed
  Before them all he takes the lead
And to follow him is no easy task
  For he always has something in a flask

And when the otter it gets slain
  He takes the road to catch a train
Oon that day the train was late,
  So Archie had an hour or so to wait
And with some auld wives he had a tussle
  When Bob, the Bellman, played his whussel.
In Day's auld smiddy near the line,
  The name of the place you a'ken fine,
With one auld wife he wheeled and cleeked
  Until he fairly swat and reeked
But Bob, the Bellman, was yet to please
  So he doffed his hat for some bawbees,
Then Bobby, he went whussling up the raw
  While Archie on the guid wives made a ca'
And when the bawbees at him they were popping
  He smiling, bowed and tugged his topping.
And when into Bob's hand he did them count
  It was full five bob they did amount,
Now quote Bob 'This day we've done no ill
  We'll be the better of another gill,'
But a single drap they could not drain
  So off they went to catch the train.
And now my country friend, I'll gie a tip,
  Just call on Archie Steel an' have a nip,
And get it out the bottle labelled with M.D.
  It stands upon the shelf as you may see,
Then ask to see his museum
  For it is really worth your while to see'em
There's Silver Pheasants and White Craws,
  Sparrow Hawks, Cushies and Pie Maws,
Humming Birds, Nightingales and Cock-a-toos,
  Parrots, Plovers, Sandpipers and Cuckoos,
Foxes, Weasels, Ferrets and Pole-cats,
  Kangaroos, Badgers, Beavers and White rats,
Peasweeps, Water hens, Bats and Banty Cocks,
  And an auld blunderbuss that wants the locks
As it had been at the wars when they were rife
  And faith, it nearly cost auld Nick his life
For Archie once at him he had it cocked
  When ower the dyke he quickly popped.
There's silver medals, jugs and cups
Won by 'Kelso Beauty' or her pups,

And lots of birds both large and small
  It's not in my power to name them all
So no longer on them will I dwell
You can go and see them for yoursel,
And now my kind and dainty friend
  This note to you I must really end
I expect to see you at the Crailing games
  But guidsake dinna try to hang the wains
For last year you made their gabs to gape,
  And nearly cut their thropple with the tape
I hope this finds you well and going about
  Though your getting auld without a doubt.
  But lang may it be before you have trouble
  But lang, lang may you the wifie cuddle
And when it comes your last breath you have to draw,
  May you be a great great-grand papa,
  And now I will stop my ranting rhyme to you,
And for the present time will say Adieu.

THE DANDIE IN AMERICA

The Dandie Dinmont Terrier was known in the United States as early as 1886. There is a record in the American Kennel Club Stud Book of three being registered in that year, imports from Scotland by Mr. and Mrs. John E. Naylor of Chicago, Ill. All were peppers—the dog, Bonnie Briton, and two bitches, Pansy and Pride of Leader. Pansy was recorded as a show winner just prior to her registration at shows in Chicago, New Orleans and Milwaukee. A year later, a mustard dog, King o' the Heather, was imported by Edward Brooks of Boston, Mass. This dog later became a Champion, the first American Champion Dandie.

Between 1908 and 1928 twenty-one Dandie Dinmont Champions were reported, most of them in the ownership of Alfred B. Maclay of the Killearn Kennels. Apparently, a club was formed for the breed in this period with a Mrs. G. Foster-Rawlins as secretary, but records seem to be lost. Dandie interest livened up in 1928 with Mr. and Mrs. J. B. Scott ('Carthagena'), Mr. R. Stockton White and his daughter, now Mrs. L. Illoway ('Buccleuch') and Miss Esther Bird, later to be Mrs. G. Plunkett ('Heatherden') playing an active part with their dogs in the show ring. In February 1932, due to the enthusiasm of these people, the Dandie Dinmont Terrier Club of America was formed and held its first meeting.

The believed first American-bred Dandie Champions were from the 'Buccleuch' Kennels—Auld Pepper o' the Ark and Auld Nick, bitch and dog respectively, both being made up in 1931. In 1932 the club's inaugural specialty show was promoted at Greenwich with an import by Harry T. Peters—Ch. Alexander of Clane O'-Windholme being best of breed, the same dog winning it again the following year. In 1934 Buster of Carthagena, an American-bred dog owned by the Scotts won the award, the 1935 event being taken by Mrs. R. H. Johnston's Ch. Seale Twinkletoes. The 'hat trick' was achieved in following years by Mrs. S. A. Gayley's Ch. Bellmead Dreamer, followed by 'Heatherden' Kennels winning with Ch. Alpin Noah three years running. In 1942 Mrs. Gardner's American-bred Ch. Keeper of Kiltmine won the last Best of Breed before the war stopped further specialties being held. When these events were recommenced in 1948 'Heatherden' won with Ch. Heatherden Irresistible. Later, in 1953 and 1955, Int. Ch. Weir of Waterbeck, litter brother of Ch. Waterbeck Watermark and owned by Mr. and Mrs. Wm. W. Brainard, Jnr, of the 'Downsbragh' Kennels won the now much sought-after award. In 1956 and for the following two years, a son of Watermark referred to above won the specialties. This was Int. Ch. Salismore Silversand owned by Dr. M. J. Deubler's 'Glespin' Kennels. The 1959 specialty was won by Ch. Cliffield Galashiels and Mrs. A. E. Johnston's Ch. Glespin B. Brown won the 1960 award. These were the early days of the breed from its start in the States into more modern years. Today, a big number of Dandies enjoy show-going and the breed seems a very popular one in America. There is a 'Dandie of the Year' award by the club and this is decided by assessment of 'Trophy Points' awarded to individual exhibits. The Dandies who win such an accolade have every reason to be regarded as top exhibits in the American fancy. The 1970 winner was Ch. Lacherbie Jolly Elf of Dowell owned by Mrs. S. L. Dowell, an extensively exhibited Dandie in the Western States. Unfortunately, he died suddenly soon after receiving the award. A list of the notable winners who have contributed to the history of the Dandie in America is too lengthy to be encompassed by this book. However, details of award winners can be obtained from the secretary of this thriving club—Dr. M. Josephine Deubler, whose address can be found at the end of this book.

THE AMERICAN STANDARD

This varies but little from the English document, the differences being mainly in wording. However, a qualifying section has been added to Mouth, the bite being described as: 'The incisors in each jaw are evenly spaced and six in number, with the upper incisors over-lapping the lower incisors in a tight scissors bite.'

In 1971, the D.D.T.C.A. adopted an official statement on Movement. It should be made clear that although this is *not* incorporated in the breed Standard, it is being distributed to all judges and publicised as much as possible. It reads:

'*Proper movement requires a free and easy stride, reaching forward with the front legs and driving with evident force from the rear. The legs move in a straight plane from shoulder to pad (allowing for a turnout of the front feet) and hip to pad, with the pads being placed progressively closer to a centre line as the speed increases. A stiff, stilted, hopping or weaving gait and lack of drive in the rear quarters are faults to be penalised.*'

Certainly, movement is a difficult thing to describe. It is possible that the foregoing will need 'fashioning' before it is understood completely in relation to the Dandie Dinmont Terrier. Of course, the best way to know whether one is moving right is to draw on instinct which comes from experience. If you have had good Dandies running around you for a year or so—you soon know whether a dog is moving correctly for his breed.

Trimming is another art which the Americans have developed to a point which some British fanciers are apt to view as extreme. *Correct* trimming is done by plucking and drawing using only the fingers and thumb. The knife should never be used and no coat which has been 'attacked' by the stripping knife can be properly judged for texture. This is because the pencilling has been lost by the undercoat and harsher coat being cut or clipped to the same length. Although many American owners put their dogs down in the show ring impeccably trimmed, there seems still a wide divergence of trimming method in practice. The Club stresses the importance of reading Cook's monograph on the breed, pages 104–9 from which valuable advice will be gleaned on matters of coat. Quite a few exhibits have too much undercoat, others boast 'skirts' perhaps reminiscent of the Skye Terrier. However, these features are receiving the club's close attention and no doubt will soon be rectified where the need arises.

The D.D.T.C.A. have formulated a Code of Ethics for their members. This is a highly commendable digest which clubs concerned even with other breeds would do well to emulate. It sets a high standard in dogdom and its objectives are clearly to benefit the Dandie. Details are given below:

THE DANDIE DINMONT TERRIER CLUB OF AMERICA

CODE OF ETHICS

The objectives of the Club shall be:

(*a*) to encourage and promote the breeding of pure-bred Dandie Dinmont Terriers and to do all possible to bring their natural qualities to perfection;

(*b*) to urge members and breeders to accept the Standard of the Breed adopted by the Club and approved by the American Kennel Club as the only standard of excellence by which Dandie Dinmont Terriers shall be judged;

(*c*) to do all in its power to protect and advance the interests of the breed by encouraging sportsmanlike competition at dog shows.

Some of the principles necessary to attain our objectives, compliance with which is expected:

Each member who contemplates breeding a litter, or who allows the use of his stud dog to the same end, shall direct his efforts toward producing Dandies of exceptional quality.

No dog showing a serious defect in type, structure or temperament shall be offered at stud. Likewise, owners of stud dogs shall not accept for breeding any bitch, the reproduction of which is likely to be detrimental to the breed.

Ch. "Sowdens Penelope", owned by Mrs. H. D. Jameson.

group of early 'Bellmead' Dandies owned by Miss Trefusis-Forbes, founder of the kennel.

The Hon. Mrs S. McDonnell's "Darenth Junerose" (puppy) Ch. "Darenth Janey", "Darenth Juldi" and Ch. "Darenth Jacintha".

Mrs. Vere Sage's Ch. "Hamish of Clane" and Ch. "Hasty of Clane". *Photo: Fall*

Mrs. M. L. Chandler's "Gossip of Gardenside".

Mrs. Leycester-Penrhyn with some the 'Clane' Dandies, 1932.

Major C. Hall Parlby's "Salismore Monybuie". *Photo: Cooke*

Mrs. Janet Lee Gordon's Chs. "Howcaple Jean", "Howcaple Mustard", "St. Conal's J

Dandie Sports Day at 'Bellmead' 1930. Start of the Flat Race.

Ch. Hatton Redcap, owned by the late Miss R. Whitelaw.

Mrs. P. Salisbury's Ch. "Salismore Mermaid".

Ch. Shrimpney Sunstar, owned by Miss C. M. Dandison .*Photo: Fall*

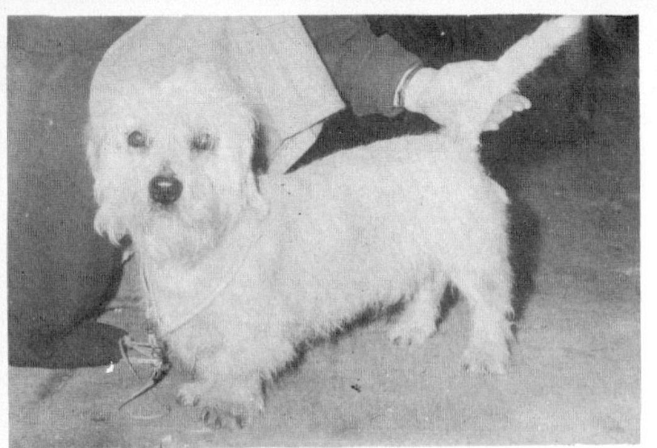

Mr. Murray Gate's
"Craigvar Crystal".

Ch. "Alpin Crisis" bred by
Mrs. T. M. Simpson-Shaw.

Mrs. P. Hulme's Ch.
"Hendell Pippin".

Mrs. P. Salisbury's Ch.
"Salismore Melrose".

Mrs. B. A. Sullivan's Ch. "Dandyhow Wizaburn
Vixen". *Photo: Roslin-Williams*

Mrs. P. Salisbury's Ch.
"Salismore Mischief".

J. A. M. Henderson's
"Elmbank Nell".

Dr. J. A. Wilson's Ch. "Glassford Craigvar
Covergirl".

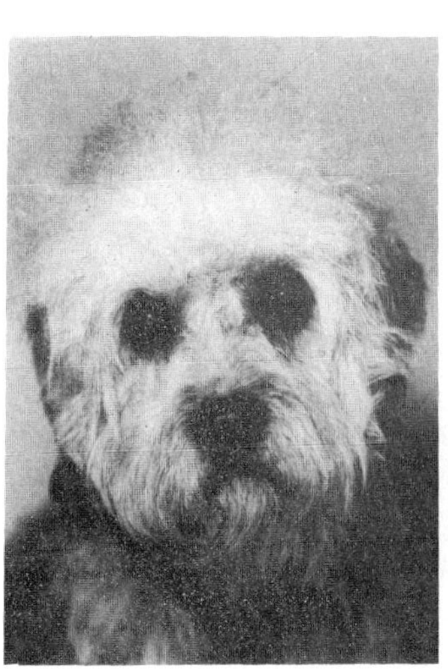

Mrs. C. A. Miles' Ch.
"Bellmead Frost".

Mrs. Janet L. Gordon's Ch.
"Howcaple Jean".

Miss R. Whitelaw's Ch.
"Hatton Numbus".

Ch. Gladsmuir Gay Goddess, owned by Mr. G. J. Johnston.

Ch. Drevaburn Falloch owned by Miss F. E. Soutter and Miss M. E. Greenlees
Photo: Reid

Mr. John Jardine trimming a Dandie Dinmont.

Miss J. Trefusis-Forbes (Founder of the 'Bellmead' kennel) with some Dandies at a 1930 dog show.

Mrs. P. Salisbury's Ch. "Salismore Scattercash".

Windsor show 1953.
Mrs. P. Salisbury's Ch. "Salismore Parsley" and Mrs. C. A. Miles' Ch. "Bellmead Dominant". Judge Mrs. I. Trotter. *Photo Cooke*

Mrs. Oliver's Am. & Can. Ch. "Shrimpney Scarlet Star".

Mr. George Jardine, founder of the 'Waterbeck' kennel and his daughter, with two Dandies.

Some of the gathering with dogs at the Restoration of Dandie Dinmont's tombstone at Oxnam Cemetery, 1969. *Photo: Clapperton, Selkirk*

Am. Ch. "Woodbourn Fancy Free", note U.S. Winner, owne by Mr. and Mrs John Davies, Jnr. c Ohic

"Bonnie of Clane" returning home with a trophy.

If a dog or bitch has produced any offspring with serious defects detrimental to the animal's well-being, such as blindness, deafness, lameness or impairment of the vital functions, and produces like results with a different mating partner, the owner shall refrain from further use of this animal for breeding. A bitch shall be bred more often than two out of three heat seasons, then only if she is in robust health; and never at the time of her first season, unless this occurs after 12 months of age.

No member of this Club shall engage in the wholesaling of litters of Dandie Dinmont Terriers or the selling of Dandies to such places as pet dealers, catalogue houses or similar sources of distribution.

No member shall engage in the breeding of his own bitches for profit without regard for quality.

Price of puppies, adults and stud services shall be based on individual quality. All puppies and adults shall be sold in a clean and healthy condition and shall be old enough to make the necessary adjustments to a new home safely. No adult or puppy shall be sold without adequate protection against disease.

When a Dandie (puppy or adult) has a serious deviation from the standard which makes it unsuitable for breeding is sold, it is the obligation of the seller to so inform the buyer. The buyer should also be told that the Dandie is being sold with the understanding that it should not be shown or bred. The breeder and the buyer should have signed statements to this effect.

No member shall engage in false or misleading advertising or other misrepresentations of his Dandies; nor shall he malign his competitors by making false or misleading statements regarding his competitors' Dandies, breeding practices or person.

Each member of the Club has an obligation to protect the interests of the breed by conducting himself in a manner designed to reflect credit on himself, his breed and on the Dandie Dinmont Terrier Club of America.

To those who yearn only for a Dandie as a companion, he is ideal, for his friendliness, kindness, loyalty and unity in ownership are established virtues in his make-up. He is wise to a degree, quiet enough until he has to guard, dignified and yet gay. His keen eye takes in everything about him and his even keener ear gives ample warning of distant approach. Perhaps a little 'bossy' and stubborn at times he is a dog who 'minds his own business' at all times and although he will take a restrained but thoroughly dignified and respectful interest in his owner's human friends, he will be ready to leap to his master's or mistress's aid at a second's notice. He is, in fact, the true 'big-little' dog and as such can be relied upon to enter into family life with understanding.

5

Breeding

THE production of pure-bred dogs conforming as near as possible to the current breed Standard should be the aim of every Dandie Dinmont Terrier breeder. Not only is this the most fascinating pursuit of a breeder's activity, but a contribution to the general improvement of the breed. It is true enough that the average breeder's knowledge of genetics is sparse (in some cases non-existent), but by careful practice and observation he can obtain some useful knowledge which will aid him in his efforts to perfect his stock.

Probably the best method of establishing a greater degree of lasting quality in one's stock is of line breeding. Line breeding is substantially identical with close inbreeding, but it takes appreciably longer to establish purity of strain. It has far less risk attached to it, and is a better and safer procedure for the breeder who cannot afford to reject a high percentage of the stock he produces in the early establishment of his strain. This includes the following crosses: cousin to cousin, grand-dam to grandson, and grandsire to granddaughter. In this, one ancestor would appear twice in the previous three generations, but not within the last two. The term is frequently extended to include pedigrees in which one ancestor appears twice within the last five generations. All such breeding must be conducted with the utmost care to prevent undesirable latent characteristics from rising to the top and getting the upper hand, thereby leading to atavism or reversion to much earlier type.

Once a pure strain has been evolved little can be done in the matter of improving it if the breeder continues to mate within his own stock. Some of the old Dandie breeders, because of too much conservatism in their breeding, found this out to their cost. Care

Table Showing When a Bitch is Due to Whelp

Served Jan.	Whelps March	Served Feb.	Whelps April	Served March	Whelps May	Served April	Whelps June	Served May	Whelps July	Served June	Whelps Aug.	Served July	Whelps Sept.	Served Aug.	Whelps Oct.	Served Sept.	Whelps Nov.	Served Oct.	Whelps Dec.	Served Nov.	Whelps Jan.	Served Dec.	Whelps Feb
1	5	1	5	1	3	1	3	1	3	1	3	1	2	1	3	1	3	1	3	1	3	1	2
2	6	2	6	2	4	2	4	2	4	2	4	2	3	2	4	2	4	2	4	2	4	2	3
3	7	3	7	3	5	3	5	3	5	3	5	3	4	3	5	3	5	3	5	3	5	3	4
4	8	4	8	4	6	4	6	4	6	4	6	4	5	4	6	4	6	4	6	4	6	4	5
5	9	5	9	5	7	5	7	5	7	5	7	5	6	5	7	5	7	5	7	5	7	5	6
6	10	6	10	6	8	6	8	6	8	6	8	6	7	6	8	6	8	6	8	6	8	6	7
7	11	7	11	7	9	7	9	7	9	7	9	7	8	7	9	7	9	7	9	7	9	7	8
8	12	8	12	8	10	8	10	8	10	8	10	8	9	8	10	8	10	8	10	8	10	8	9
9	13	9	13	9	11	9	11	9	11	9	11	9	10	9	11	9	11	9	11	9	11	9	10
10	14	10	14	10	12	10	12	10	12	10	12	10	11	10	12	10	12	10	12	10	12	10	11
11	15	11	15	11	13	11	13	11	13	11	13	11	12	11	13	11	13	11	13	11	13	11	12
12	16	12	16	12	14	12	14	12	14	12	14	12	13	12	14	12	14	12	14	12	14	12	13
13	17	13	17	13	15	13	15	13	15	13	15	13	14	13	15	13	15	13	15	13	15	13	14
14	18	14	18	14	16	14	16	14	16	14	16	14	15	14	16	14	16	14	16	14	16	14	15
15	19	15	19	15	17	15	17	15	17	15	17	15	16	15	17	15	17	15	17	15	17	15	16
16	20	16	20	16	18	16	18	16	18	16	18	16	17	16	18	16	18	16	18	16	18	16	17
17	21	17	21	17	19	17	19	17	19	17	19	17	18	17	19	17	19	17	19	17	19	17	18
18	22	18	22	18	20	18	20	18	20	18	20	18	19	18	20	18	20	18	20	18	20	18	19
19	23	19	23	19	21	19	21	19	21	19	21	19	20	19	21	19	21	19	21	19	21	19	20
20	24	20	24	20	22	20	22	20	22	20	22	20	21	20	22	20	22	20	22	20	22	20	21
21	25	21	25	21	23	21	23	21	23	21	23	21	22	21	23	21	23	21	23	21	23	21	22
22	26	22	26	22	24	22	24	22	24	22	24	22	23	22	24	22	24	22	24	22	24	22	23
23	27	23	27	23	25	23	25	23	25	23	25	23	24	23	25	23	25	23	25	23	25	23	24
24	28	24	28	24	26	24	26	24	26	24	26	24	25	24	26	24	26	24	26	24	26	24	25
25	29	25	29	25	27	25	27	25	27	25	27	25	26	25	27	25	27	25	27	25	27	25	26
26	30	26	30	26	28	26	28	26	28	26	28	26	27	26	28	26	28	26	28	26	28	26	27
27	31	27	1	27	29	27	29	27	29	27	29	27	28	27	29	27	29	27	29	27	29	27	28
28	1	28	2	28	20	28	30	28	30	28	30	28	29	28	30	28	30	28	30	28	30	28	1
29	2	29	3	29	31	29	1	29	31	29	31	29	30	29	31	29	1	29	31	29	31	29	2
30	3			30	1	30	2	30	1	30	1	30	1	30	1	30	2	30	1	30	1	30	3
31	4			31	2			31	2			31	2	31	2			31	2			31	4

must be taken, however, when introducing new blood to closely examine its effects. It is far better to use a sire whose work in the breeding field has been irrefutably established than take a chance on a cheaper and untried youngster whose efforts may well ruin in a few years a line which has taken a lifetime to perfect.

No two dogs are identical even though they may be of the same close gene construction and when slight variations in pure lines are noted, it is usually atributable to varied environments, the ordinary process of selection having little effect upon them. Dogs who evince the effects of undesirable mutations must be disposed of at once, for only the use of those who can maintain the standard of the strain should be kept.

The beginner's first lesson in the work should be to thoroughly apply himself to learning the breed Standard and understanding its significance in relation to the living dog. He should attend as many local shows, especially championship shows, as he can manage. Here he should watch the judging and form his own conclusions as to the relative merits of the competing dogs, and discuss their points with breeders present. The leading Dandie kennels should be visited, and there he will usually be well received by the breeders and helped with his problems and queries. Most Dandie Dinmont Terrier breeders are ready and eager to help the newcomer with sound advice, and much can be learnt from the right people.

It should not be forgotten, however, that the formation of a leading strain has usually entailed many years of hard work with its inevitable disappointments, and whatever information is gleaned from these experts is of high value to the novice who is thus able to utilize it and avoid the pitfalls ordinarily lying in his own path. Whatever is learnt should be gratefully acknowledged, but I do not suggest that every chance remark heard at shows should be accepted as gospel; and the novice must learn to distinguish between opinions and facts.

Most successful breeders have what is termed 'an eye for a dog'. This sense (it is almost a gift) does not come to everyone, but those who have it invariably have many years of experience in their breed and rely implicitly upon this instinct when making their decisions. Of course, it does not necessarily follow that all those who have been connected with Dandie Dinmonts for thirty years or more are better able to assess a dog's true points than the man who has only a few years' experience to his credit, for the latter may have studied his subject deeper and with greater acumen, but there is little doubt that length of practical association with a breed sharpens the eye as to what constitutes a good dog of a given type. This method of appraisal is normally used by eminent breeders when selecting mating pairs and conforms to the old and well established, if sometimes controversial law, that 'like begets like'.

This assumes that when two parents of a similar type are mated together their progeny will be of that same type, and provided this is supported by efficient line breeding based on a clear picture of the parents' ancestry as far back as possible, then successful breeding should be ensured.

To begin then, you find a dog and bitch who resemble each other structurally, and are good Dandie Dinmont Terriers in themselves with no glaring faults, are sound anatomically and in perfect health. The idealist will go even further; he will study their pedigrees as well and so ensure that they in their turn are the progeny of good parents and grandparents, thus increasing his chance of producing good stock of the same type. In fact it is important to every breeder to do his best to pick parents with pedigrees as good looking in their way as the animals themselves.

It will be found that the majority of puppies bred from two similar parents will inherit much of the characteristics of both sire and dam, yet there will be some youngsters in the litter who do not conform to this rule, and may not even resemble either parent. For example, presuming that both parents excel in head properties then most of the puppies will have good heads, but there *may* be a few in the litter who are weak in heads. These are throw-backs to an early ancestor about whom you probably had no information, and the characteristics which thus appear in an otherwise uniform litter represent tendencies which may be apparent or latent, and transmitted in subsequent generations.

When dissimilar types of dogs are bred together, some puppies will tend to follow the type of one parent, and some the other, with possibly one or two falling midway between the two. These latter, should they prove worth-while specimens (which is rare), will be of little use for breeding, for they will be likely to pass on to their own progeny the undesirable features of their own parents. Thus, it will be seen that the more detailed your knowledge of the animals which go to make up your dogs' pedigrees, the better your chances of success in the breeding field, provided this knowledge is intelligently applied.

CHOOSING A BITCH

It is important that the beginner should buy the best bitch he can afford, and it should never be thought that the brood bitch's points and conformation are of secondary importance. For successful breeding, of course, it is important to choose a good sire, but it is *infinitely* more important to have a good dam.

Whereas with a good bitch one might easily breed some excellent stock with a more ordinary stud dog, the best of sires cannot be expected to achieve much with a plain bitch. Never be deluded into believing that one can successfully breed good stock from poor bitches. It is true that there have been cases where rather poor dams have produced winning stock, but these are exceptions, and it must be apparent to any intelligent person that the poor bitch with the good-looking offspring represents a 'black mark' in the pedigree of her progeny, who will in all likeliness throw back to her in their own litters. Thus, although the owner of such a bitch may congratulate himself on having improved the type of his stock, he may find that this is only a temporary advance.

The commonly recognised course of inheritance is tail-male, which totally disregards the female lines in the pedigree, possibly because the task of planning a breeding programme is made easier in view of the greater number of offspring from a male enabling the planner to assess better his worth as a sire, whereas the progeny of a bitch is necessarily limited. For this reason the undoubted importance of breeding tail-female is generally overlooked, which is unfortunate, for it is one of the most important factors in breeding to type, as without good bitches to breed to good dogs, no real or permanent advance can ever be made.

Having briefly stressed the importance of the bitch, let us consider how you buy her. If you cannot afford a worthy Champion bitch, then you should buy a grown bitch as free from faults in her make and type as possible. Her pedigree is important too, and this must be studied closely to ensure that her immediate ancestors do not carry faults likely to be transmitted. If, then, her close ancestry shows dogs known to have been (*a*) badly undershot, (*b*) badly overshot, (*c*) single-coated, (*d*) very light-boned, (*e*) light in eye, (*f*) poor in tail carriage, (*g*) bad in pigmentation, then reconsider your choice, as she is useless to any conscientious breeder, for these are serious transmittable faults.

The bitch must possess correct temperament, a good head and coat, typical dark eye (high-set and slit eyes are an abomination), sufficient bone, long, strong and flexible body, wide pelvis and broad beam with correct tail carriage and free movement. It is also important that she should be feminine; in the same way as you would detest a bitchy dog, avoid a doggy bitch, for such are likely to produce coarse stock.

The next point for consideration is her mothering capacity. If she is bought as a maiden, then only time will tell, but if she has already had litters, then satisfy yourself by tactful inquiries as to how she raised them. A bad mother can be a worry and expense, as well as possibly begetting daughters who will be poor mothers in their turn.

The second alternative if you have little money is to buy a bitch puppy of the choicest breeding and rear it yourself. The points to look for in a puppy of say three months are: (*a*) dark, well-placed eye, (*b*) longish neck and good shoulders, (*c*) well-set tail, (*d*) level mouth, (*e*) deep stop and rather short foreface, (*f*) 'quality'—difficult to define, but very necessary.

CHOOSING A SIRE

The breeder should never be swayed unduly by show records, which possibly may not possess the worth attributed to them. It has been known for a Champion to win his title in mediocre competition and it is for this reason that I have advised a regular attendance at shows. Here we can study specimens in open competition and the true worth of a dog's wins can be assessed.

You may have a really good bitch, but she will not be without some slight faults, and your aim will be to correct these deficiencies in her progeny. For example, there is a belief that if a bitch is rather high on the leg, she should be mated to a dog extra low on the leg using the theory that one extreme will effectively cancel out the other. This is entirely incorrect, for you would be virtually mating one fault to another fault, and the result would be shown in a litter which would contain some puppies who were too high on the leg (taking after their dam), and some too short (after their sire). You may by this method produce an *occasional* puppy who falls midway between the two parental types and stands the correct and desired height from the ground, but that puppy on maturity would not constitute in himself a good breeding proposition, for he would carry the tendency to transmit *both* his parents' faults to his own progeny. The bitch should, in this instance, be mated to a dog who stands the *correct* height from the ground, then as some puppies tend to resemble either parent, you would get several youngsters standing at the correct height. These in their turn would carry the tendency to transmit only *one* fault (legginess) and not *two* faults (legginess and shortness).

The foregoing illustrates only one example, but the sense of it may just as easily be applied to any pair of opposite characteristics.

Always choose a dog who is in himself a real Dandie and is reproducing his own excellent type . . . you can check this by examining litters he has got by other bitches. His temperament must be correct too: we have leading dogs who do not possess the true Dandie temperament, but have won their awards in the show ring under judges who do not realise the urgent need of maintaining this prized characteristic. The dog to use is he who suits the breeding of your bitch, is himself as near perfection as possible, and whose ancestry is beyond reproach. He must be masculine and full of fire, and sound in health and constitution. Do not rush to sires merely because they are Champions. There are probably worthier dogs out of the rings you attend than in them, either for reasons of their owners' inability to visit the big shows or their lack of interest in exhibiting.

COLOUR

The pepper and mustard colours peculiar to the Dandie Dinmont find equal favour with breeders and the public. Both colours can, of course, occur in one litter, even if both parents are mustards, seldom, however, if they are peppers. To get good colours in a litter it is advisable to mate pepper to mustard or vice versa. It is important to keep coat colours distinct. In the early days of the breed 'saddlebacks' were quite common, but were not encouraged and today are seldom if ever seen. 'Saddlebacks' are peppers with too much mustard or mustards with too much pepper infiltration, normally on the back of the animal.

MATING

As is commonly known, a bitch's period of oestrum or season is between sixteen and twenty-one days. No definite time for mating can be given as animals vary considerably, but the best time is usually when the coloured discharge has ceased for a day or two. Some bitches will take a dog at any time between the tenth and fifteenth day, but others have to be caught at a certain time, sometimes within a few hours. If your bitch tends this way have her kennelled near a stud dog during her vital period so that she can be introduced to him immediately she shows willing. From my own experience, I have found that the average bitch is ready for mating at any time on the twelfth or thirteenth day of her season.

Should you not be using your own dog to her, it is advisable to accompany the bitch to the stud rather than send her alone. By so doing, you will save her possible distress at a critical period, and at the same time ensure that the mating was successful with the dog of your choice. The best time for mating is early morning, both dog and bitch having been allowed plenty of time to empty themselves prior to the union. Neither animal should have been fed for at least twelve hours previously.

If your bitch is a maiden and you are using an experienced stud dog you should have little cause to worry on the successful outcome of the affair, for the dog will normally conduct matters efficiently. If, however, her mate is to be an untried dog, then care must be taken. The mating should be attended by two handlers, and one of these must at least have previous knowledge of the procedure. The bitch's owner should hold her collar firmly and the other handler must support her loins at the same time directing the dog in his task with encouraging words and manipulative assistance if necessary. For those who have inexperienced potential stud dogs it is always advisable to get them used to manipulative handling from the start of their first affair. In difficult cases a handler's assistance and co-operation is expected and appreciated by the trained stud. A dog should have his first bitch when about ten months of age, then no more until at least fifteen months. Always endeavour to find him an experienced matron for his first mating.

Some breeders prefer what they term a 'natural' mating, and

this entails both animals being left alone to effect copulation without any outside assistance. This, of course, is an admirable thing if it can be done, but unfortunately natural matings are seldom effected without some distress to either animal, and for this reason I prefer a closely supervised mating. Most pedigree dogs have a high monetary value, and Dandies or not, tough as they may be, there is little sense in leaving the two to run in a paddock and returning later to find slit ears, gashed eyes or at worst ruptured stud. Such calamities can occur easily, even between a couple who normally run together and are usually the best of friends.

The dog's natural instinct will cause him to take the initiative in the mating and once he has entered the bitch he should be held for a few moments until a tie has been effected, this being conclusive evidence that the seminal fluid is being deposited. In a small handbook like this we need not go into the mechanics of this device of Nature, nor need we deal with its complications. I might add that not all breeds tie, and not all individual dogs effect a tie, and although this action is not essential, it gives greater confidence to the owners if it can be effected.

Copulation usually lasts between fifteen and twenty minutes during which time the animals have doubtless brought themselves round tail to tail, or have been eased round to this position by the handlers, but this aid should not be attempted until it is certain that the two are firmly locked. Both dogs should be held quite firmly during the operation, care being taken that the bitch is not allowed to drag the dog or to roll over, and this should be continued until the dog disengages from the union. They should then be removed from each other's presence and adequately fed, watered and rested. The dog's personal comfort should be attended to by ensuring that the sheath covering the penis has returned to its natural position. One service is usually sufficient, and a second is not required from a dog regularly at stud

THE BITCH IN WHELP

It is important to see that the bitch in whelp is kept in the prime of condition throughout her pregnancy. It is a vital period for her, and for her puppies, and the owner should ensure that she maintains a perfect bloom.

The normal time for a bitch to carry her young is considered to be sixty-three days, but the puppies may be a few days earlier or later. Her exercise should be normal up to the last fortnight after which she should be taken on slow walks. Jumping, rough play and any stresses should be severely discouraged. Her feeding should be sufficient to nourish and build her well for the vital period. Extra nourishment such as calcium phosphate or calcium lactate, cod-liver oil, dried brewer's yeast, tomato juice and other rich sources are invaluable, not only for the bitch herself, but to aid bone and tissue formation and general development in the puppies. (See whelping chart on page 90.)

About ten days before she is due to whelp, give a daily *small* teaspoonful of medicinal paraffin, to oil her up nicely inside and to keep her bowels open. Just before she is actually due to whelp, reduce her food a little and stagger the feeds, for distension must be avoided.

The bitch about to whelp should be provided with suitable quarters, and a whelping box such as the one here illustrated will allow her to have her puppies in comfort, and at the same time let the owner attend her without difficulty.

The box in my sketch is similar in type to those used in the best whelping kennels. The 'pig-rail' shown is a valuable, and in my opinion, an essential adjunct, and has prevented many pups from being squashed by clumsy bitches. It should allow ample room for the puppy to rest under the shelf in safety with the bitch leaning against it. The drop-front allows the control of their comings and goings. The measurements given can, of course, be adapted.

Some breeders do without any bedding at whelping time, but the best and safer plan is to use a clean, disinfected piece of sacking (hessian or crash material will do) fastened *securely* and stretched tightly to the entire base of the box with strong flat-headed nails. A bitch will always scratch during labour and it is quite easy for loose bedding to become folded and envelop the whelps. Thick layers of hay or straw should be avoided for the same reason. Considering the Dandie's big bone, short forearm and long arched body, with most of the weight being thrown on to the foreparts, the breeder should ensure that puppies are kept on a perfectly level floor with no steps or inclines.

WHELPING

The bitch should have been introduced to her new sleeping quarters at least a fortnight prior to whelping, so that a sudden change does not distress her and cause complications at the later stages. If you intend to see the matter through yourself you will need a small first-aid kit by you. What this constitutes depends largely on your experience and what you consider necessary. As a guide, the following are necessary components to this kit:

1. A new packet of soft paper napkins or 8-in. squares of surgical lint.
2. A pair of sharp, sterilised, probe-pointed, surgical scissors.
3. Some lengths of surgical thread or strong cotton.
4. Dettol.
5. T.C.P. or similar disinfectant.
6. Vaseline.
7. Some clean pieces of towelling.
8. A *covered* hot water bottle, preferably a stone one.
9. A feeding bottle.
10. A little brandy and a small teaspoon. If this has to be used, only a few drops should be given.

The bitch will have gone off her food just prior to being ready to whelp. This is normal and need not cause alarm. She will have become rather fretful and anxious, and will frequently jerk her head round to her rear end—an indication that the first puppy is on the move. At this stage, labour is imminent and she should be watched constantly. Whelping usually commences with noticeable muscular contractions, and possibly some panting. At this point, she may be given a little warm milk to drink, but it is far better to let the bitch proceed without interference of any kind. On the other hand, if the bitch is already very late in her term, and the labour seems to be going a lot longer than one's peace of mind allows, then it is best to call in qualified veterinary advice at once.

Puppies are born one by one, each puppy in its own membraneous sac. They are usually presented head first, but occasionally the rear end will arrive first; a situation which need not cause alarm, unless the bitch seems to be in distress in which case she

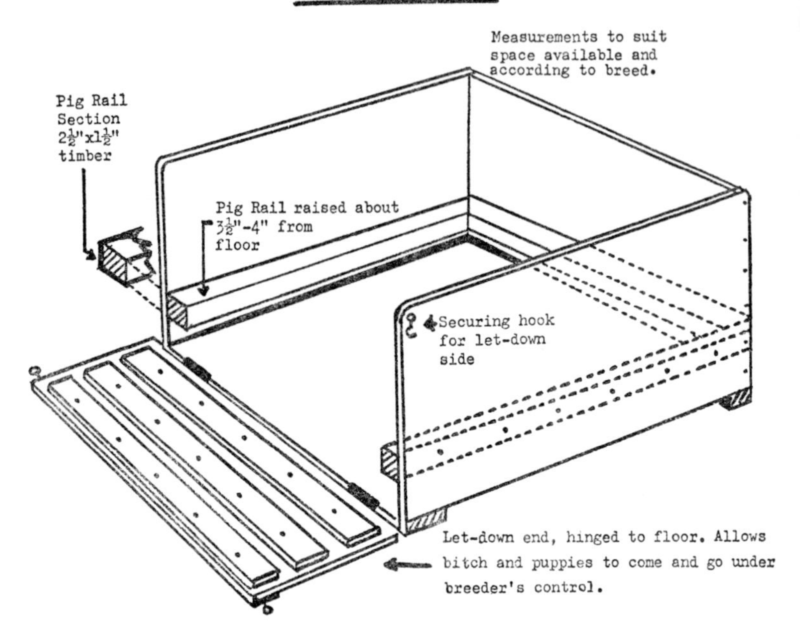

will need assistance. However, whelpings are best not meddled with, and if a natural whelping is achieved it is better for all concerned.

A maiden bitch may be bemused at what is happening to her, and appear not to have the slightest idea how to proceed when the first puppy shows itself. If she seems exhausted, and is making no effort to deliver her first-born, the whelp can be gently gripped with one of the pieces of towelling you have ready, and eased out carefully in rhythm with the strains. A bitch should release the puppy from the protective sac herself, nip the umbilical cord and clean up, but here again if her reactions are slow, and it seems necessary to help her, the breeder can achieve the work for her with scissors and lint. Care should be taken that no tension is put on the cord, or umbilical hernia in the puppy can result.

An afterbirth follows each puppy, and this is at times actually eaten by the bitch. Such a thing need cause no horror in the minds of novice breeders for it is a natural action inherited from the wild state when it would form an emergency meal. However, some controversy exists on the advisability of allowing this, for domestic animals are not fitted for the habit as are their wild cousins, and biliousness may result. However, it is a relatively unimportant point, and is mentioned to save the owner any worry should the bitch so dispose of the afterbirth.

Should it prove necessary to nip the cord to assist the bitch, cut it deftly about one and a half inches clear of the puppy's navel over a tie made firmly and tightly around with a piece of the surgical thread, thus forming a ligature. This may have to be done with the first puppy of a maiden bitch, but even the rawest mothers soon find that their instinct will draw them to do all the work themselves and achieve this with teeth and tongue.

Puppies are born fairly quickly in succession, and it is important to see that the final puppy is followed by its afterbirth. If this does not come away entirely in a reasonable time, there could be some danger of infection. In any case, should some afterbirth remain, veterinary advice is indicated.

After whelping has been completed, the bitch should be encouraged away from her family out into the garden to relieve herself. The puppies can then be examined for their sexes and signs of any abnormalities, and the box made presentable and clean for her return. She will begin to suckle the pups almost at once. Watch the puppies carefully and make sure the strong and greedy ones do not hog all the milk.

The groin or inguinal teats give the most plenteous supply, and it should be seen as far as possible that all the puppies take their turn here. Ensure that the dam is well fed and watered, for her body now has added responsibilities. Plenty of liquids are indicated to make milk for her charges and to encourage a ready flow.

The dew-claws should be removed from the puppies about four days after they are born. You can instruct your veterinary surgeon to do this job for you, or if you prefer to complete the task yourself it can be done with ordinary sharp scissors, being sure to sterilise the wounds afterwards.

I have tried to cover a lengthy subject as briefly as possible while giving the main facts of this fascinating procedure, which after all should be the desire of any self-respecting breeder to see through on his own as far as possible. However, there are some who are a little excitable or nervous, and for these it is advisable to have their veterinary surgeon in attendance.

Peppers when born are black-and-tan, occasionally a slatey-blue; mustards, a dirty brown or clean golden. The smooth black-and-tans, although looking puny against pups that have a rough greyish coat, are more likely to meet requirements as the latter frequently turn out with too profuse coats of soft texture. Mouths should be level. Sometimes puppies have uneven mouths, and there is a chance that these may correct themselves as they get older, but this is rare.

6

Feeding

WEANING

WEANING can commence when the puppies are three weeks old by teaching them to lap Lactol (or similar preparation) twice daily. At first the quantity given should be very small, and in fact there need be no rush to get them to drink milk other than their mother's for there is no milk quite so good for them. However, the best proprietary brands of milk have much to commend them, and they should be warmed just to blood heat.

The bitch herself may later aid in the weaning process by disgorging half-digested food for her puppies to eat. Once they have learned to lap and eat, they may be put on slightly firmer foods within a few days, such as light milk puddings, a little poached egg, and later some minced boiled tripe and finely shredded raw meat, moistened with a little cod-liver oil. It should be obvious that *only* butcher's meat should be given to puppies at this stage, and if for some reason this is not available, the meat must be boiled.

By the fourth week, the puppies should be taking half their feed from their mother, and the rest from the dish. The solids should have been gradually increased, but note that it is important to stagger the feed to the extent of about six feeds daily by the time they are six weeks old. Steamed fish is of high protein value, and crumbled rusky wholemeal bread is excellent. This can be usefully mixed in with the fish or raw meat meal. By this time they should be entirely self-dependent, and only allowed to the mother for brief visits if she is in need of it, at least until she is dried out.

Goat's milk is a most useful aid to the rearing of young puppies, in view of its high fat and mineral salts content. Cow's milk is good, but of secondary value, and should never be diluted.

At two months of age, the puppies can have minced meat rather than shredded pieces, using only lean raw meat. Small lumps should be cut, and to this can be added raw carrots or the liquid from cooked endives and turnip tops, both rich in iodine and mineral salts. Ordinary vegetables should not be fed to a puppy under six months of age. A little liver may be added to the programme, but this again should be raw unless the puppies show some looseness in their motions when cooked liver is better.

At this age it is as well to give the feeds at regular intervals, say at 7 a.m., 10 a.m., 1 p.m., 4 p.m., 7 p.m., and 10 p.m. all in quite small quantities to avoid any distension of the stomach muscles. Later, as the puppies progress in age, a mealtime can be excluded, and the six mealtimes so made into five, and proportioned out regularly throughout the day. By the time they are say three months old they should be on not more than four meals, the times adapted to suit your own convenience.

Regularity of feeding is important and once you have settled on feeding times they should be maintained. A suggested feeding programme for young puppies of this age is given herewith:

8.30 a.m. Bread and milk, cereal and milk, Robinson's Groats, etc. The milk should be just warm, never hot.

12.30 p.m. Chopped meat meal with warm gravy made from Oxo, Bovril or broth. This can be mixed with wholemeal or brown bread rusks soaked in the gravy or in boiled vegetable liquid.

4.30 p.m. A warm milk meal, or rusks soaked in gravy or vegetable liquid.

8.30 p.m. Repeat the meat meal exactly as for the 12.30 p.m. meal.

Remember the value of raw eggs in particular, these being great body builders. Vitamin B is contained in dried brewer's yeast and is most valuable to the youngsters. Iron is found in the proprietary Parrish's chemical food, and in Easton's syrup, but moderation in these should be observed due to the rather constipating effects. Powdered calcium obtainable from the chemist or on veterinary prescription can do much for bone development.

Honey too in its natural form is a great boon, especially to sickly puppies and adults. Good makes of biscuits should not go unheeded, and will fulfil the starch requirements of the average puppy, but I prefer the use of oven-baked wholemeal bread, barley and maize meal.

ADULT FEEDING

From the age of seven months the forward puppy can virtually be fed as an adult. It is best to give him a light meal at midday of a little meat and a few biscuits; the main meal being better given rather late in the evening *after* his exercise or work in the field, so that he can gain the full nutritive effects from his food which will be correctly digested while he sleeps. A Dandie should always be fed dry—soft mushy food is useless for good results. He should never be either fed or watered after heavy exertions such as a ratting expedition, but should be allowed to settle first.

To give him an occasional change from raw meat, he can have steamed fish which has been carefully boned or herrings fed raw, which are excellent for his coat and general health. If he can have a rabbit immediately after it has been killed, he will gain much from it, but rabbit bones are dangerous when the animal has been dead a day or so.

Poultry bones should never be given to a dog. The only bones permissible are the big marrow or knuckle bones, and even these should be avoided if you are cultivating a show dog who evinces a tendency towards an undershot jaw.

During winter months, a teaspoonful of coarse cod-liver or halibut oil should be given each evening. Malt extract is a great body builder too, but in the summer months he had better have pure olive oil.

An adult Dandie Dinmont should have *at least* ½ lb of fresh raw meat daily. If you are forced to allow him less than this the balance should be made up with some other form of nourishing food. It should be remembered that it is a mistake to economise in feeding, for a well-fed dog in good condition is a prized possession, and the little extras you may have to spend on him will strengthen his resistance to disease and probably save you quite a lot of money in veterinary expenses.

7
General Management

CONTROL

THE genuine Dandie Dinmont Terrier has a mind of his own in that he knows what he wants to do, and intends to do it. However, he is readily adaptable to the home as he is to the kennel or the field, and will respond amiably to intelligent control. His training in the home should be kind but firm, and if you have had your dog from puppyhood, and he remains out of hand, this reflects upon your aptitude as a trainer. From the start, the youngster must be taught the meaning of the word 'No' and it will be found that most puppies are anxious and willing to learn. A puppy must *never* be thrashed as apart from the ethics of the matter, he will lose confidence in you and will never respond to training.

The Dandie is quite an easy subject to train in cleanliness. As a very small puppy when he relieves himself indoors he does not know that he is doing wrong. Pick him up, show him the little puddle and put him near to it, so that he can comprehend the reason for your scolding. Then put him outside into the garden, provided the weather is sufficiently clement, and say just one short word like 'Out' and sure enough you will find that after constant repetition of this procedure he will walk of his own accord to the door which leads outside when he feels the call. Encourage him and praise him and in a very short time you will have a house-clean puppy. Remember though, if you are not around to catch him in time or to open the door for him you must not scold him, for that would be unfair.

As a house dog, the Dandie is an excellent guard, giving ample warning of strangers, and his bark, so deep and loud for such a small dog, can prove a useful deterrent to unwanted visitors. He is naturally a good watchdog, inclined at times perhaps to be a mite too keen if not controlled, but sensible restraint to his enthusiasm will always have the desired effect. It is not considered advisable to keep two of the same sex together without supervision.

KENNELLING

Never kennel a dog if you can possibly accommodate him with the family circle. As I have said, the average Dandie Dinmont Terrier constitutes a good watchdog, guarding not only property but persons with his life, and he is better fitted to fulfil this function in the home than he will be locked up in a kennel. Likewise, a dog who is allowed to mix freely with humans becomes far more lovable and intelligent than the kennel dog who virtually leads a life of solitary confinement, broken only by the occasional visit of his owner or at feeding times and the only-too-brief periods of exercise.

However, where a number of dogs are maintained, kennel arrangements are indispensable, although it should be added that to get the best out of each dog, he should be allowed in the home for a few hours daily. For the kennels themselves, it is wise to buy the best you can afford or at least in keeping with the name and quality of your stock.

There are several excellent makes of pre-fabricated sectional kennels on the market, and these can be bought, quite reasonably, even today. A range of four, with possibly an end-section to house straw and kennel equipment, is a useful size for the small breeder. It is advisable also to have one kennel placed well away from the main range to be used as a sick-bay if needed. Individual kennels should be fairly spacious as no dog thrives in cramped quarters. They should stand at least six feet high to enable the owner to stand inside with comfort. An outdoor run should be fitted to each kennel, and sixteen square feet space for each inside kennel is ideal, with a six-foot run, bounded on all sides with strong link fencing. Cement runs are bad for puppies; small cinders being better.

Should you decide to build your own kennels, rather than buy them, it is advisable to study the designs of professionally built models before proceeding. Sleeping benches should be raised well up from the floor of the kennel, as draughty quarters endanger health, and are in fact largely contributory to debility in kennel inmates. These sleeping benches should slide out or be otherwise detachable to allow easy cleaning of the main kennel. Each dog must have a constant supply of fresh water within easy reach and attention to dryness and cleanliness every day constitutes the essence of kennel hygiene.

Positioning of kennels needs care and thought. You should select a spot which is not overhung with foliage which will drip for hours after every shower. The area should allow a free passage of sunlight and pure air, and the whole structure should be built on a well-drained soil (gravel or sandy soil is best) facing south or south-west and away from the prevailing winds of the district if possible.

Of course, as your stock increases and you find it becomes necessary to enlarge the kennels your equipment and appointments become more extensive. Then it is a matter of separate day and night quarters, an exercise paddock, a special outhouse for cooking, and a dry store for foodstuffs and the like. An entire book could be written on the detailed management of such an establishment, which would fall more into the professional field and is beyond the bounds of this book.

EXERCISE

Exercise is the second important need in the life of a dog, the first, of course, being feeding. It is best to exercise the very young puppy in the garden until his body has gained some resistance to disease but later when he is old enough to go on the lead he should be walked daily. Do not allow him to put his weight against the lead, for this will tend to throw out his shoulders and spoil his movement.

The Dandie needs far more exercise than is suggested by the length of his legs. His muscles must be maintained in sound condition with adequate exercise, and vigorous play and clambering is vital in toning up the body and system. I am a great believer in walking dogs on the lead, preferably over hard ground, for several miles a day. In my opinion it makes for better general condition than does uncontrolled exercise. The hard ground will tighten up the feet, and strengthen the pasterns, while the steady rhythm of walking benefits the body generally. Of course, the dog needs to chase a ball and enjoy himself, and to indulge occasionally his fancies by the hedgerows, so he should have his fair share of these pleasures to offset the dull routine of the lead.

If your dog gets very wet, either in the rain or in swimming, at which the Dandie is an expert, he should be dried down thoroughly when home. His coat is very protective but precautions are better than cures, and many domestic animals have not the same constitutions as their working brothers. Above all never allow your dog to get fat, for fat Dandies are an abhorrence.

GROOMING

This should be a daily routine. The Dandie needs quite a harsh brush to get the best results with his coat, and remove all loose hair. It is as well to get the dog used to grooming right from puppyhood. If this is done, he will begin to enjoy the daily session on the table. Begin with a coarse comb behind the ears, coming down all over the body, and down the legs to the feet, making sure that you do not miss the hair inside the legs, and on the underside of the body. Comb the tail, and see that all is clean beneath it. Remove at once any dried excreta which may be there by careful trimming with scissors.

Attend to the dog's nails if this is needed. Actually, it should not be necessary if the dog is a young one, for exercise should have kept the nails down to their correct length.

Inspect the insides of the ears to make sure that they are healthy and there is no inflammation present. Check on eyes and nose for any unusual discharge. Look inside the mouth to see that all is well with the teeth. If the dog is kennelled on straw you will have gone through the coat to remove any fleas or lice which might be present, and given the body a light dusting with a proprietary anti-parasite powder.

Do not bathe the Dandie unless his coat is in such a mess for some reason or other as to really warrant it, as frequent bathing softens the coat texture.

TRIMMING

In the past, trimming and titivating the Dandie has sometimes approached the notorious, the head and face in particular coming in for more than their fair share of the hairdresser's misdirected art. What should have been achieved by careful selection and breeding has been done with finger and thumb or at worst the clippers. Whereas it is important to make the best of the Dandie, the travesties of trimming sometimes seen achieve only the opposite effect and if continued may well spoil the victim's coat for ever.

Not every breed requires trimming or attention to its coat apart from the usual and essential daily brushing and grooming. Many owners seldom bother about trimming for effect, but in the show ring a detailed attention to the coat and various points of the dog is necessary. Much can be achieved with the Dandie by subtle trimming to accentuate his good points and to improve visually upon those points in which he may be deficient as an individual.

For those who are interested in this subject—and every owner should wish to make the most of his Dandie—here is a brief routine on trimming. It should be noted that all the work, with the exception of minor details of finishing, is done with finger and thumb. Clippers and scissors should not be used in the *main* work.

Body

Taking first the coat, about eight weeks or more before the date of the show, remove most of the old hair from the top coat only. The Dandie's coat is at its best when about 1½ in. to 2 in. long, so work to this. Do not interfere with the undercoat. The *Neck and Shoulders* should be trimmed carefully between the second and third weeks prior to the show.

Ears

About two weeks before the show, trim the ears, leaving the hair at the top of the ears to be combed to join the top-knot. This will give an effect of added width to the head. Leave a good inch of hair tapering to the tip of the ears where the 'tassel' hangs down.

Remove all the hair from the underside of the ear, which will allow the ear to hang down very close to the cheek.

Nose and Muzzle

Clear all the long hair from the nose to the stop, taking care to make it close. Remove the hair in the crevice or dip between the eyes to accentuate the stop, but do not remove the hair too high up towards the forehead.

Eyes

Trim under the eyes, removing all superfluous hair. This will enhance their beauty and largeness. Care must be taken not to overdo this trimming, and to give time for the 'spectacles' to re-furnish or the expression of the dog will be marred.

Forelegs

The forelegs should be cleared of most of the long hair at the front and inner sides only, leaving a slight 'feathering' towards the back of the legs.

Hind Legs and Rear Parts

The hind legs should be cleared of all long hair from the hocks to the ground. Tidy the hair which ranges from the base of the set-on of the tail right down to the hocks.

Tail

The tail should be thick at the base, tapering to a point. All hair beyond the bone of the tail should be carefully and lightly taken off with a stripping knife, but preferably with finger and thumb, taking pains to taper it naturally. Remove all hair which is wispy and superfluous to the natural feathering.

Feet

Tidy the feet to look round and neat. Cut the nails should this be necessary, being sure not to damage the cuticle.

Underbody

Trim the underbody with a stripping knife or finger and thumb from the end of the ribs to the hind legs in order to show a carefully graduated and natural cut-up of loin and shapely waist.

Head

The top-knot is the Dandie's crowning glory, and deserves especial care and attention. The top-knot should be trimmed to give a rounded effect. All wispy, untidy hair should be fore-shortened with the finger and thumb only a day or so before the show, and many enthusiasts will whiten it for added effect with a little chalk and powder but be sure to remove all chalk before entering the ring or you will lose the silvery sheen. Comb it up-wards from the neck, and get it to stand softly all over the head, but clear of the eyes.

In conclusion, avoid bathing the coat just prior to the show as this will tend to soften its texture which must be crisp to the touch. A daily good hard brushing of the body using a little rain water, some weeks before the show and leading up to it will do much to improve the appearance and feel of the coat.

AILMENTS

I do not intend to attempt a list of ailments common to the dog, mainly for the reason that in the first place I do not believe that I can conscientiously cover the subject in the space allotted for the purpose, and secondly because I consider that such matters are better left to qualified veterinary practitioners. A little knowledge in the hands of the layman can be ill-used, not deliberately, but because experience is needed in the matters of correct diagnosis and prescribed treatment.

Every owner should observe the natural precautions in the care of his puppy and its protection from disease. The puppy should not be allowed to sniff at street corners and lamp-posts where dangerous germs may be lurking. The dog should be kept in the peak of condition at all times, especial care being taken when the puppy's resistance is at its lowest—during the teething period. In this way, the dog will have maximum resistance against disease, especially those complaints which normally attack the under-nourished dog. Immunisation against distemper and its kindred perils can be done by a qualified veterinary surgeon when a puppy is three months old, earlier in some instances. This is essential as a safeguard to the well-being of your dog.

'Slipped' Discs

This is a condition while certainly not confined to Dandies is a hazard in the breed. In spite of the fact that the well-reared Dandie Dinmont Terrier is a strong and physically competent dog; by virtue of his spine's conformation and its length and flexibility, he can—in common with certain other long-backed breeds prove subject to vertebrae trouble. This can take the form of what is sometimes termed 'P.I.D.' (Prolapsed Intervertebral Disc) or just plain 'Slipped Disc'. It can be contracted by any dog, caused by just an involuntary movement or more likely by enforced body pressure on the spine when the body is placed at an unfavourable angle. It is less likely to be experienced in a young animal than in one of veteran years, i.e. seven or more. The spinal column is made up of a series of bones, to be likened roughly to cotton reels. Between these segments lie 'cushions' of resilient gristly substance forming the 'discs'. Pressure on the spinal column can cause this material to squeeze out into the spinal cord on to nervous tissue. Sometimes the condition clears itself up quite quickly, but in serious cases the nerve(s) affected will cause disruption of the motor system, even limb paralysis and acute pain. The function of both bladder and lower bowel might be impaired and this can occur sometimes without apparent reason. A dog so affected will probably become suddenly apprehensive of fondling and being patted; some dogs change considerably in their very temperament. This in itself should constitute a warning to an astute owner. Rest and carefully applied heat treatment to the affected area will bring some relief. In some cases the application of a prescribed pain-killing drug might prove necessary, but it is better to work for a cure than just for relief in such cases. Some veterinary surgeons have considerable experience in the treatment of 'slipped' discs and it is best to consult one who has some specialist knowledge and able to suggest early and effective treatment.

8

Exhibiting

JUDGING

THE breed which is rich in competent judges is the one which will establish itself stronger in the field of pedigree dogs. Bad judging, whether inefficient or deliberate, does a great disservice not only to the exhibitor, but to the breed as a whole, and is frequently difficult to remedy.

Judging in the show ring is largely a matter of comparison, dog for dog. Prior to the issue of the current breed Standard, each breed had its own Scale of Points, which was meant to be of assistance in judging. It is clear, however, that judging by a system of points is not feasible. Proportion and breed type are the *primary* considerations in judging dogs, together with soundness, of course, and an arbitrary scale of points is useless and hindering to the efficient judge.

The Standard is the standard of perfection for the breed and tells us what the perfect Dandie Dinmont Terrier should look like. The judge *must* have a clear understanding of the Standard. Experience and, in my opinion, the possession at some time of a good one himself should aid him in forming a mental picture of the perfect Dandie. A judge's training enables him to absorb the best from every good dog he sees, and in his mind should be fixed, not just the best Dandie Dinmont he actually sees, but the best Dandie Dinmont imaginable.

When judging he must have an honest open mind, and judge a dog not on his respective lack of faults but rather according to his good points. He should avoid exaggeration in fanciers' points, and look for bone, balance, substance and soundness, not forgetting the great importance of breed character. Good movement in a dog is essential too, and showmanship should not be mistaken for quality.

All these must be reconciled with true breed type. It is difficult to define type, but broadly speaking breed type may be said to depend largely upon the anatomical structure and general appearance, whereas individual type is expressed more by points and detail.

Of course some judges differ as to their evaluation of a Dandie's points. One might emphasise the need for neck and body properties, another prefer good movement in a dog. There has been known the futile judge who will forgive almost anything if the Dandie had 'a divine expression'! No one minds legitimate preferences, but such likes and dislikes must vary within reasonable margins. In fact, if this was not so the competitive interest in showing would fade. It has been debated that one man prefers a certain type of Dandie, his companion another and different type. This is fallible argument as there can be only *one* type—the *right* type and every breeder should know it and strive for it in his work.

THE SHOW DOG

The dog for exhibition must be prepared correctly for his big day; condition must be spot-on and the dog himself should be in good mental fettle. It should be hardly necessary to mention that bitches in season should never be shown, for their effect will doubtless upset the dogs present, and maybe spoil their chances in the ring where some concentration is required to make a good appearance before the judge. Rivalry among Dandies is pretty keen in the ring, and every dog deserves a fair chance in competition, so good behaviour is important, and every owner must learn to make the best of his charge.

The dog should have been groomed and trimmed according to Dandie fashion (see section on trimming) and every effort should be made to present him soundly, and as a gay mover before the judge. If he is a bad mover, no matter how good he is in himself as a Dandie, you are unlikely to get him to the top in strong competition against those who excel in ring deportment. It is not enough to wander into the show ring with your dog on a lead and hope for the best; not many dogs show themselves naturally, and a certain amount of elementary training is necessary.

EARLY TRAINING FOR SHOW

This should commence when the dog is about five months old. Just before his evening meal, take him on his collar and lead to a quiet spot well away from the other dogs and all distraction. Have a few tit-bits in your pocket—he will be hungry, so therefore interested. Speak to him quietly and be sure that you have his confidence. A little assistance to stand 'four-square' may be given him by arranging his quarters to get him to stand nicely. At first, he will fidget a little and wonder what it is all about, but with encouragement he will gradually learn what is wanted of him when he hears the command 'Stand'.

Progress should be amply rewarded with tit-bits, and on no account lose patience with him if he is slow. Training of a puppy should never be continued for more than ten to fifteen minutes at any one time. When he has shown some prowess at this, get him to walk with you holding his lead rather slack, and yet sufficiently firmly to allow you control of the dog as he moves.

You will know that a judge must see your dog walking away from him and then walking towards him, so that he can assess among other things the exhibit's soundness and movement. This means that your dog must neither pull nor drag on the lead. An easy, free-moving Dandie with his tail gaily scimitar-wise is a joy to behold and novice exhibitors must bear this in mind when presenting their dogs.

Once your dog has proved his initial training, make him stand properly with other dogs around, and with people and strangers and other distractions around him. Encourage members of the family and visitors to open and inspect his mouth, handle his head and body and generally treat him as would a judge, and with regular practice your youngster wlll be ready for his first show.

AFTER THE SHOW

It might seem that to touch upon sportsmanship as it affects the showing of dogs is unnecessary, but unfortunately some exhibitors still have a great deal to learn of this quality. Competition is liable to cause jealousy within the ranks of its devotees, and this is, I suppose, unavoidable, so it would be a good thing if newcomers to the fancy were initiated into the accepted procedure of dog show life prior to entering their first show.

When you enter your dog in a show, you do it because you are proud of your dog, and possibly not for the sole purpose of winning a prize although to do so is very agreeable. You also wish to let the world see him and receive on him a report from a judge whose opinion you respect. Admittedly if it is your first show you do not know whether you respect the judge's opinion or not—but you usually do, and into the ring you go, full of hope and excitement.

The class over, you realise that you are among the 'also-rans'. Now you do not mind this at all, for you were there just for fun anyway, but as you stand at the ringside watching the rest of the show, you may be spoken to by a person who purports to be an 'expert' on the breed. He may tell you that your dog was an easy winner in his class and that the only reason you did not win was because the judge did not know your face. Well, human nature being what it is, you begin to wonder—and wonder. You either leave the show with self-righteous indignation, never to return, or to decide there and then to prove judge No. 1 wrong and show your dog again.

Now judge No. 1 was probably right, anyway, and although maybe he did not know your face, he was not concerned with faces anyway and being a reputable judge (most of them are) he did what he was there for . . . he judged the dogs, but just did not think that your exhibit was the sort he would like to take home.

So you show again, and maybe judge No. 2 having a class of lesser strength to judge finds a place for your dog in his awards. Now, are you going home full of his praises and announce to all and sundry that this judge is a 'straight' judge—that he knows a Dandie, and so on, thereby implying that judge No. 1 was the exact opposite?

If you feel that you might be like this, then best not bother to show, for showing dogs in such conditions becomes a headache, not only for you, but for the people around you. I am not suggesting that all judges are paragons of virtue, or enter the ring complete with haloes, but the average judge is an experienced breeder and does his best to give an honest opinion—should this not be the case, then he would not last long as a judge. Bad judges, like bad dogs and bad ringside critics soon find their own level and eventually eliminate themselves.

If every judge thought the same it would mean the end of dog shows, for the same dog would win every time. It is *individual opinion* that makes the hobby of dog-showing the interesting and enjoyable game it is, so let the newcomer go into it with an open mind and avoid like the plague all those who, prompted in the main by jealous instincts and the belief that all are swans in their kennels of geese, tend to disrupt the happy harmony of show life and the initiate's sportsmanship.

The longer you are associated with dogdom, the more you realise that the essence of the sport is to get pleasure from it, and share in the pleasure of others out of the ability to recognise a good dog, whether your own or belonging to someone else.

The old Dandie Dinmont Terrier Club Supplements, issued to members in the 1909–10 period published its 'Pointers' to Show secretaries which is good advice even today:

DON'T appoint a judge who does not know a Dandie;
DON'T appoint a judge who is known not to know a Dandie;
DON'T appoint a judge who is not known to know a Dandie;
DON'T appoint a judge who does not accept the Club Standard of Points as the true standard of excellence;
DON'T give classes for mixed sexes; dogs and bitches *can not* be judged on an equality.

It goes on to say that the support of the Club had been withheld at different times because one or other of these Dont's had been disregarded.

9
Registrations

ALTHOUGH registrations were not listed in the *Kennel Gazette* until 1880, when Volume I of that journal was issued, Dandie Dinmont Terriers had attended the shows with full pedigree honours many years previously to this, in fact well before the formation of the Kennel Club in 1873.

It was not the practice of the *Kennel Gazette* to total up their individual registrations until 1906, the same applying to the *Kennel Club Stud Book*. However, there is an interest in looking back on the annual figures for the breed, and I have been fortunate in obtaining annual registration figures for the latter part of the last century. There is no record for the years 1876–9. From 1880, therefore, the annual figures taken from January to December in each year, up to the present time, are as follows:

Year	*Total*	*Year*	*Total*	*Year*	*Total*
1880	95	1894	180	1909	144
1881	94	1895	160	1910	125
1882	116	1896	145	1911	153
1883	169	1897	160	1912	125
1884	169	1898	143	1913	116
1885	194	1899	184	1914	112
1886	241	1900	130	1915	35
1887	227	1901	147	1916	39
1888	233	1902	152	1917	13
1889	246	1903	153	1918	18
1890	207	1904	144	1919	47
1890	207	1905	182	1920	63
1891	197	1906	136	1921	86
1892	266	1907	145	1922	84
1893	143	1908	134	1923	201

Year	Total	Year	Total	Year	Total
1924	215	1940	62	1956	137
1925	296	1941	37	1957	116
1926	302	1942	60	1958	165
1927	251	1943	104	1959	183
1928	316	1943	104	1960	154
1929	346	1944	102	1961	160
1930	361	1945	135	1962	136
1931	306	1946	195	1963	195
1932	329	1947	217	1964	181
1933	344	1948	247	1965	164
1934	353	1949	185	1966	186
1935	373	1950	227	1967	176
1936	373	1951	190	1968	249
1936	417	1952	137	1969	217
1937	483	1953	129	1970	182
1938	351	1954	147	1971	208
1939	267	1955	138		

The totals speak for themselves and show periodic rises mainly between the wars. In spite of the fact that as this book is being revised registrations generally are fewer this appears due to the loss from the breed of some older breeders whose ranks have not been filled. Nevertheless there is a 'live' feeling among the enthusiastic breeders of Dandies which augurs well for the breed and its successful rise to greater popularity.

OLD PEDIGREES

Many present-day breed enthusiasts have an abiding interest in the pedigree breeding of old dogs who featured in the Dandie's historic beginnings. In *The Dandie Dinmont Terrier*, 1885 by Charles Cook, several such notabilities have their pedigrees written in the Appendix. These are reproduced herewith:

I
SHEM

Born: 1839

Description: Bluish-black-grey colour with white head; body long and arched at loins; short legs.

Owned by: Mr. F. Somner of West Morriston. Later (1845) by Mr. E. Bradshaw Smith

Weight: 14 lb. of Blackwoodhouse, Ecclefechan.

Sire: Charlie, the property of Thomas Tod, Esq., of Drygrange by Dandie I out of Shan both owned by old John Stoddart, the blacksmith from Selkirk. Stoddart was generally admitted to have the purest strain of the Dandie Dinmont breed in the Borders. Although Charlie's weight was light he had great courage and would face anything and was thoroughly tried at all sorts of vermin. Charlie's sire Stoddart's Old Dandie, was a very handsome, light grey and tan dog, with short legs. He was very broad behind. He was reputed the gamest dog of his day.

Dam: Mustard (Mr. Somner's) by Lord Polwarth's Dandie, coming from the kennel of Sir Walter Scott of Abbotsford, who presented a beautiful dog and bitch to the late Lord Polwarth of Mertoun, as specimens of the pure breed of Dandie Dinmont.

G. Dam: By one of the Marquis of Tweeddale's Terriers. The Marquis selected his own Dandies from the kennels of the best breeders in the Borders of Scotland, at long prices.

G.G. Dam: By Old Pepper. This dog was purchased by Mr. F. Somner and bred by Allan, a tinker in Yetholm famous for the purity of Dandie Dinmonts. This Allan was a grandson of old Allan the basketmaker in Hollystone, on the Coquet Water and declared Pepper to be a true lineal descendant of the famous dog Hitchem, which belonged to his grandfather.

G.G.G. Dam: By Davie, a mustard-coloured dog bred by Mr. F. Somner, later sold to the Earl of Lauderdale. Weight 13 lb only, but game enough to stand punishment from the fangs of any vermin that was taken in the traps, from a cat upwards. The gamekeepers declared that 'fear was not in his composition'. Davie was a beautiful specimen of the breed.

G.G.G.G. Dam: By Salt belonging to Mr. F. Somner. A mustard-coloured dog bred by Thomas Stevenson, Esq., Jedburgh, who had a splendid kennel of Dandie Dinmont Terriers. He was a first-rate judge of the breed and an intimate acquaintance of Mr. James Davidson of Hindlee, *alias* 'Dandie Dinmont of Charlieshope' who was one of his leading men when a day was fixed for a fox-hunt among the Cheviot Hills. Salt was about 16 lb weight and would encounter anything with a hair on't. He was sold to a nobleman at a long price, to go abroad as a perfect specimen of the breed.

G.G.G.G.G. Dam: By Wogy Cobawn bought for Mr. Somner by Mr. Stevenson out of a kennel of high repute near Jedburgh. The dog was a bluish-black colour, intermixed with white hairs, with a head covering of white hair. Head large; ears pendulous and leathery, covered with the sort of hair recommended in the Dandie Dinmont Terrier Club's Standard. He was very handsome and attracted the attention of all who saw him. This dog was larger in size than the usual run of Mr. Somner's dogs.

G.G.G.G.G.G. Dam: By Fox. This was another dog presented to Mr. Somner by Mr. Stevenson, as a stud dog. He had been a long time in Mr. Stevenson's service, bolting foxes from their strongholds in the Cheviot Hills and when given to Mr. Somner the dog's teeth were worn to stumps. When he was shown vermin he became alive for mischief. Fox was a fine specimen of the breed, having a long flexible body upon short legs. He was mated to Nettle owned by Somner, bred by James Davidson of Hindlee and produced the ancestral dam of Shem under discussion. Nettle's colour was pepper with a white head, dark hazel eyes, pendant ears, very long body upon short legs; weight 11 lb. She was very game.

All the foregoing facts were compiled from Mr. Francis Somner's notes.

II.—PEDIGREE of 'Podgy II', a Pepper Dandie Dinmont Bitch, bred by Mr. E. B. Smith of Blackwoodhouse. Whelped 1853. Died 1864.

'Podgy II.' (E. B. Smith's). (*See Illustration.*)	'Podgy I' (E. B. Smith's).	'Pepper'—Full sister to 'May-day' (see Illustration, p. 106). By 'Musty'; her dam by 'Tanner'; (Frain of Frows.) her g. dam by 'Dusty'; g.g. dam by 'Tuggem'; g.g.g. dam by 'Old Musty'. All of which were considered the pure breed'—D. M'Dougal, Cessford, 23rd June 1843.		
		'Shem.' For Pedigree see Appendix I. (F. Somner's.)		
	'Dandie (L)' (E. B. Smith's).	'Ruth' (E. B. Smith's). Bred by Hugh Purves, Leaderfoot.	'Whin'—Full sister to 'Mustard', dam of Somner's 'Shem'. (Hugh Purves, Leaderfoot.) For Pedigree see Appendix I.	
			'Dandie II'—Full brother to 'Drygrange Charlie'. For Pedigree (J. Stoddart's.) see Appendix I.	
		'Old Ginger' (E. B. Smith's). Bred at The Haining, Selkirkshire.	'Vixen' (5th Duke of Buccleuch's).	'Wasp'—Full sister to 'Drygrange Charlie'. For Pedigree see (Mrs. Douglas, Old Melrose.) Appendix I.
				'The Mertoun Dandie.' See Appendix I. (Lord Polwarth's.)
			'Old Pepper' (5th Duke of Buccleuch's).	

Note.—This Pedigree was taken from the Blackwoodhouse Records.

III.—PEDIGREE of Pepper Dandie Dinmont Dog 'Dirk' (The Incomparable). Bred by Mr. E. B. Smith. Whelped 1865. Died 1877.

- 'Dirk' (The Incomparable) (Mr. E. B. Smith's).
  - Dam, 'Jenny' (Mr E. B. Smith's).
    - 'Spice II' (E. B. Smith's).
      - 'Old Tuggem' (E. B. Smith's).
        - 'Spice I.'—Full sister to 'Ruth' ('Hugh Purves'). For Pedigree see Appendix II. (E. B. Smith's).
        - 'Dirk I' (E. B. Smith's).
          - 'Pepper' (Frain's). For Pedigree see Appendix II.
          - 'Dandie II.'—Brother to 'Drygrange Charlie.' (J. Stoddart's.) For Pedigree see Appendix I.
      - Dandie (L.) For Pedigree see Appendix II. (E. B. Smith's).
    - 'Jock.'—Full brother to 'Dandie (B.)', whose Pedigree see below. (E. B. Smith's.)
  - Sire, 'Pepper' (Mr. E. B. Smith's).
    - 'Fanny' (E. B. Smith's).
      - 'Tot' (E. B. Smithls).
        - 'Venom (B.)' (E. B. Smith's).
          - 'Wasp' (Duke of Buccleuch's).
            - 'Shan' (Duke of Buccleuch's). Full sister to 'Drygrange Charlie.' See App. I.
            - 'Pepper' (Duke of Buccleuch's).
          - 'John Pym' (Dr. Brown, Melrose). See Pedigree below.
        - 'Dandie (L.)' For Pedigree see Appendix II. (E. B. Smith's).
      - 'Ginger' (E. B. Smith's).
        - 'Old Tuggem' (E. B. Smith's).
          - Spice I.—Full sister to Ruth', for whose Pedigree see Appendix II. (E. B. Smith's.)
          - 'Dirk I.' (E. B. Smith's).
            - 'Pepper' (Frain of Trows.) For Pedigree see Appendix II.
            - 'Dandie II.' For Pedigree see App. II. (J. Stoddart's.)
        - Dandie (L.) For Pedigree see Appendix II. (E. B. Smith's).
    - 'Dandie (B.)' 'Dandie (B.)' (E. B. Smith's).
      - 'Jenny' (Nicol Milne of Faldonside).
        - Pepper bitch.
        - Yellow dog.
        - Both belonging to Ned Dunn, Whitelea, a hunting companion of James Davidson, Hindlee.
      - 'John Pym' (Dr. Brown, Melrose).
        - Bitch (John Lauder, Bemerside).
          - 'Pepper' (Frain of Trows). For Pedigree see App. II
          - 'The Teviotfoot Dandie.'
        - 'Shem' (F. Somner's). For Pedigree see Appendix I.

Note.—This Pedigree was taken from the Blackwoodhouse Records.

IV.—PEDIGREE of Pepper Dandie Dinmont Dog 'TWEEDMOUTH', belonging to T. F. Slater, Carlisle, and bred by the late Mr. J. Robertson, Belzies, near Lochma[illegible]
Whelped January 1879.

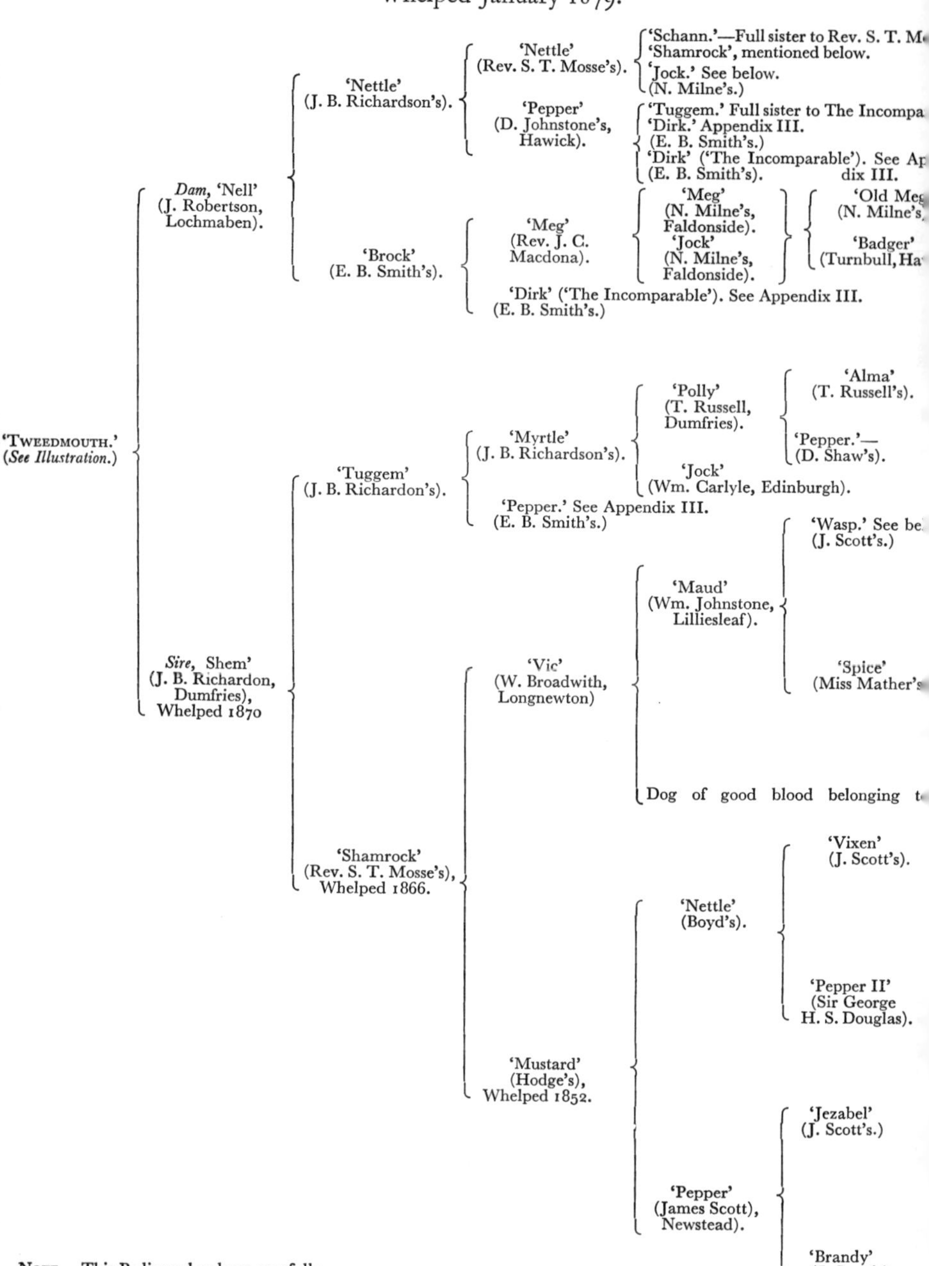

NOTE.—This Pedigree has been carefully verified from the Blackwoodhouse Records, and other documentary evidence produced.

ıbull's bitch from Kyle of Braidlea

ɔie' (Frain of Trows).

ıugg' (T. Russell's). — 'Nettle.'—From Wm. Carlyle, Edinburgh. (T. Russell's). / 'Dandie' (Mr. Lyon, Kirkmichael). — 'Shan' (J. Stoddart's). / 'Dandie I.' (J. Stoddart's). — See Appendix I.

ɛrry.'—Bred by Marquis of Abercorn.
Marshland, Glenae).
ɣ E. B. Smith, and same blood as his Pepper'.

ɬe Spice' Scotts). — 'Spice' (Johnstone's). — 'Nettle' (Brisbane's). / 'Pepper' (Sir George Douglas).
'Brandy.' See below. (Jas. Scott's.)

ɔod's Dog ɛngrove, ɐberland). — 'Viper' (E. B. Smith). — 'Wasp' (E. B. Smith). — 'Tib' (Pringle of The Haining). / Dandie' Pringle of The Haining). — Sister and Brother — 'Wasp' (Mrs. Douglas), Sister to Drygrange 'Charlie.' App. I. / 'Dandie' (Lord Polwarth's). See Appendix I.
'Hitchen' (E. B. Smith). By 'Shem', Appendix I, out of 'May-day', Appendix II.
'Dirk I.' See Appendix III. (E. B. Smith).

at Piershill Barracks.
ɒice.'—Bred by M'Dougall, Cessford.
ɪbane's.)

ɛpper' bane's). — 'Nettle.'—Bred by Mr. Lyon of Kirkmichael. (Brisbane's).
'Demon' (Brisbane's). — 'Pepper' (John Reid's), who at an early period had his Terriers from James Davidson. / Friar Tuck.' (Frain of Trows. Bred by Mr. Oliphant, Marlfield.)

'Schann' ɜeorge Douglas). — "Schann.'—Sister to Drygrange 'Charlie'. See Appnedix I. (Duke of Buccleuch's). / 'Pepper' (Duke of Buccleuch's).

'Pepper I.' Bred by Mr. Lang.
George Douglas.)

ess' cott's). — 'Mustard.' See below. (J. Scott's.) / 'Old Pepper.'—*Sire*, 'The Slater' (Wat. Leithead), accidentally shot in 1833. Colour grey and tan. Died very old about 1842. Bred by Mr. Taylor, Whitelea. (Sir G. Douglas.)

ʎasp' cott's). — 'Vic' (J. Scott's). / 'Pepper' (J. Scott's).

ʎasp' cott's). — Nettle' (J. Scott's). — 'Ringlet.'—A grand-daughter of (J. Scott's). Lord Polwarth's 'Dandie' 'Dandie.' (Duke of Buccleuch's). — 'Miss Whisker' (J. Scott's). — 'Wasp' (J. Scott's). — 'Wasp' (Mr. Sitwell, Barmour). / 'The Slater' (Wat. Leithead). / 'Dandie' (Lord Polwarth's). / Dandie' (Rev. T. Thomson, MaxtontManse). See Appendix I
'Dandie' (J. Scott's). — 'Mustard.'—Descended from 'The Slater' and Lord Polwarth's 'Dandie.' (J. Scott's). / Drygrange 'Charlie.' See Appendix I.

ɪck.'—Bred by Henry Dodd.—*Sire*, 'Pepper;' *Dam*, 'May-day,.
Brown.

V.—PEDIGREE of Pepper Dandie Dinmont Terrier Bitch 'Border Queen'. The propery of Mr. W. E. Easten, Hull. Bred by Mr. William Foster, Carlisle. Whelped 11th June 1877. Weight, 19 lb.

'Border Queen.' (*See Illustration.*)	*Dam*, 'Ruby' (Mr. Foster's, Carlisle).	'Nettle.' See Appendix IV. (Mr. J. B. Richardson's.)	
		'Shem.' See Appendix IV. (Mr. J. B. Richardson's.)	
	Sire, 'Davie' Mr. Redford, (Silloth).	'Tatters' (Mr. E. B. Smith's).	'Brock' (Mr. E. B. Smith's). — 'Fanny.' See Appendix III. (Mr. E. B. Smith's.)
			'Brock' (Mr. E. B. Smith's). — 'Jock.' Brother to 'Dandie (B).' See Appendix IV. (Mr. E. B. Smith's.)
			'Boxer' (Mr. E. B. Smith's). — 'Old Tuggem.' See Appendix III. (Mr. E. B. Smith's.)
			'Boxer' (Mr. E. B. Smith's). — 'Dandie (L.).' See Appendix II. (Mr. E. B. Smith's.)
		'Dirk' (The Incomparable). See Appendix III. (Mr. E. B. Smith's.)	

Note.—This Pedigree has been verified from the Blackwoodhouse Records ,and other documentary evidence produced.

GLOSSARY OF TERMS

AFFIX. Term given to a kennel name which is attached to either end of a dog's name to identify him with the particular kennel, The Kennel Club require actual *Breeders* of the dog or its parents to put their Affix *before* the registered name, while *non-Breeders* of the dog should put their Affix *after* the dog's registered name. The Kennel Club has waived this rule until 1st January, 1976, for Affix-holders who compounded their kennel name before 1st January, 1971, and applied to the K.C. Committee for permission to be free from the positional limitations.

APPLE HEAD. One with the skull rounded on top as in Toy Spaniels.

ARCH. In the Dandie Dinmont this should take the form of a slight upward curve over the loin only.

BARRELLED. Pertaining to the ribs which are strong and well rounded, allowing plenty of heart room.

BAT-EARS. Large erect ears like those of the French Bulldog.

B.B. Best of Breed. A dog who has beaten all others of his breed.

BLAZE. A white (usually bulbous) marking running up the centre of the head.

BLOOM. Glossiness or good sheen of coat.

BONE. A well-boned dog is one possessing limbs giving an appearance and feel of strength and spring without being coarse.

BR. Breeder, that is, the owner of the dog's dam at the time of whelping.

BRACE. Two dogs exhibited together.

BRINDLE. A mixture of dark and light hairs giving a general dark effect, usually being lighter streaks on a grey, tawny, brown or black background.

BRISKET. That part of the body in front of the chest and between the forelegs.

B.S. Best in Show, or Best in Sex. A dog who has beaten all others, or all others of his sex, respectively.

BUTTERFLY NOSE. When the nostrils are mottled or show flesh colour amongst the black pigment.

BUTTON-EARS. Ears which drop over in front covering the inner cavity, as in the Fox Terrier.

CAT-FEET. Short, round and deep feet, well held together.

C.C. Challenge Certificate. A Kennel Club award signed by a judge for the best dog of his sex in breed at a championship show.

CH. Champion. The holder of three C.Cs. awarded and signed by three different judges.

CHARACTER. A combination of the essential points of appearance and disposition contributing to the particular variety of dog to which the holder belongs.

CLODDY. A low and very thick-set build.

CLOSE COUPLED. Short or closely knit between the fore and hind limb joints.

COBBY. Of compact, neat and muscular formation . . . like a cob horse.

CORKY. Compact, nimble in body and mind, lively and spirited.

COUPLINGS. That part of the body between the fore and hind limb joints.

COW-HOCKED. A dog is said to be cow-hocked when his hocks are bent inwards, thus throwing the hind feet outwards. A fault in any breed, even the Pyrenean Mountain Dog and present-day St. Bernard.

CREST. The upper part of a dog's neck.

CROUP. The area adjacent to the sacrum and immediately before the root of the tail.

DAM. The female parent of puppies. The term is generally used but has special reference to a bitch from the time of her whelping a litter to the weaning of her last puppy in that litter.

DEW-CLAWS. The rudimentary fifth digits and claws found on the insides of the leg below the hocks which are better removed a few days after birth.

DEWLAP. The loose pendulous skin under the throat.

DOWN-FACED. May be briefly described as a bending or curving downward of the top line of a dog's face when viewed in profile.

DOWN IN PASTERN. Showing an angle of the front feet forward and outward instead of the correct pastern (straight in line from the forearm to the ground).

DUDLEY NOSE. Nostrils usually wholly cherry or coffee-coloured; distinct from the Butterfly Nose.

FLY-EARS. Semi-erect ears which stand out from the side of the head.

FRINGES. The long featherings on the ears, the backs of the legs and thighs, and on the tail.

FRONT. Strictly speaking all that can be seen from the front except the head, but having special reference to the soundness of brisket and forelegs.

GAY TAIL. One which from root to tip is carried above the horizontal.

GOOD DOER. A dog who does well without any special treatment and has thrived from birth.

GRIZZLE. An iron-grey colour.

HARE FEET. Feet which are rather long and narrow with the toes well separated, like those of a hare.

HAW. The inner part of the lower eyelid, which is well developed, hanging open and shows red in such breeds as the St. Bernard and Bloodhound.

HEAT. A bitch is said to be on or in 'heat' during her oestral period, when she is in 'season'.

HEIGHT. Usually measured perpendicularly from the ground to the top of the shoulders.

HOCKS. The joints in the hind legs between the pasterns and the stifles.

INBREEDING. The planned mating of related dogs in order to perpetuate certain characteristics which may be desirable, and which already exist to some extent in the blood of the dogs concerned.

INT. CH. International Champion. A dog who has been awarded Championship status in more than one country.

LEATHER. The skin of the ear flap.

LEGGY. So high on the leg that the dog appears asymmetrical.

LEVEL JAWS. When the jaws are so placed that the teeth meet about evenly, neither undershot nor noticeably overshot.

LIPPY. When the lips are developed, or overhang more than is correct.

LOADING. Heaviness in shoulders.

LOINS. That part of the body protecting the lower viscera. Between the last ribs and hindquarters.

LONG COUPLED. Reverse to close coupled.

LUMBER. A dog having lumber is one with too much flesh, ungainly in appearance and clumsy in action. Not to be confused with the gawkiness of puppies.

MAIDEN. In the widest sense an unmated bitch, but in exhibition language usually a dog or bitch not having won a first prize.

MASK. The dark marking on the muzzle, or the muzzle itself.

MATCH. A form of competition which is usually arranged more or less privately by which members of local and breed societies can meet, discuss and compare special points in specimens presented.

MATRON. A brood bitch. One kept for breeding purposes.

MUZZLE. The projecting part of the head combining the mouth and nose.

N.A.F. Name applied for.

N.F.C. Not for competition.

OCCIPUT. That part of the skull at the top of the back of the head which is prominent in most of the Hound group.

OESTRUM. The menstrual period. A bitch experiencing oestral flow is said to be 'on heat' or 'in season', that is, she is sexually excited and ripe for service by a male dog.

OUT AT ELBOWS. Having the elbow joints noticeably turned away from the body.

OUT AT SHOULDERS. Having the shoulders protruding outwards so as to increase the width of the front, as in the Bulldog. A bad fault in the Dandie and synonymous with loose shoulders.

OVERSHOT. Having the upper incisors projecting over and beyond the lower incisors.

P. Puppy.

PAD. The cushioned sole of the foot.

PASTERN. The lowest part of the leg, below the knee on the foreleg or below the hock on the hind leg.

PEAK. The term applied to the occiput when it is prominent, but rightly restricted to use with Bloodhounds, Basset Hounds and many Setters.

PREFIX. An obsolete term for Affix.

RACY. Long-bodied and slight in build, as in the Whippet.

RANGY. Rather long in body but having more substance than a racy dog.

RED. Strictly speaking this is a general term for several colours, ranging from fawn to copper red.

RESERVE. Usually the fourth place after judging, that is the fourth best exhibit, though it may be the runner-up in any class.

RIBBED UP. A compact dog with the ribs nicely placed and developed.

RING TAIL. A curled tail which describes almost a circle.

ROACH BACK. One which arches upwards from the withers along the spine with particular emphasis about the loins.

SADDLEBACK. A faulty rendering of colour mixture, i.e. a pepper with too much tan, coming up over the back giving the impression of a pepper coat mounted with a mustard saddle and vice versa.

SECOND MOUTH. A dog has his second mouth when the first or milk teeth are replaced by the second or permanent teeth.

SECOND THIGHS. The muscular development of the leg between the stifle and the hock.

SERVICE. A mating. The act of copulation when a bitch is served by a stud dog. A 'free service' is one given by courtesy of the owner of the stud following an unsuccessful mating for which a fee had been paid.

SET-ON. Where the root of the tail is set on to the body.

SNIPY. When the dog's muzzle is weak, and too long and narrow.

SPLAY FEET. Those of which the toes are set wide apart.

SPRING. Elasticity. Spring of rib is when the ribs are well rounded, sound and elastic: spring of back means its ability to return to its normal level after pressure away from that level.

STERN. The tail. A term which should be restricted to sporting circles. Stern-high is used to describe a topline which is in a straight line from withers to stern.

STIFLE. The joint in the hind leg joining the first and second thighs, and corresponding to the human knee.

STOP. The depression between and in front of the eyes.

SUFFIX. When a kennel name, e.g. 'Watersend' is written *after* a dog's name, e.g. Ch. Sage *of Watersend* it is said to be used as a Suffix.

T.A.F. Transfer applied for.

THROATY. When the skin is too loose at the throat.

TOP-KNOT. The long fluffy 'powder-puff' hair on the head of the Dandie Dinmont and Bedlington Terriers.

TRANSFER. A change of ownership of a dog which is registered with the Kennel Club, duly reported, paid for and recorded.

TUCKED-UP. When the loins are lifted well up, as in the Greyhound group.

TYPE. That quality essential to a dog if he is to represent or approximate the ideal model of his breed based upon the Standard desired in that breed as drawn up by a body of recognized experts: a dog who 'has type' is therefore one who though not necessarily perfect embodies much of the ideal—conversely a dog 'lacking type' is one who though possibly possessing several good points is a long way from being a living model of the ideal.

UNDERSHOT. Having the lower incisors projecting beyond the upper, due to a malformation of the jaws as in the Bulldog.

UNSOUND. An unsound dog is one who is unhealthy, or below average in general condition, working ability, movement or character. The unsoundness may be temporary or permanent, partial or complete: a bitch after whelping is temporarily unsound by being out of coat, etc.; a deformed or unreliable dog is more or less permanently unsound.

WEEDY. Very lightly formed and lacking in substance.

WELL-SPRUNG. Well formed, with particular emphasis on chest development and spring of rib.

WHEEL BACK. Another term for roach back, an arched or convex back.

WITHERS. That point between the shoulders where the neck joins the body.

BREED CLUBS AND THEIR SECRETARIES

THE DANDIE DINMONT TERRIER CLUB: G. Murray Gate, Esq., 109 Leeds Road, Ilkley, Yorkshire.

THE SOUTHERN DANDIE DINMONT TERRIER CLUB: Mrs. H. D. Jameson, 'Sowdens', Stogursey, Nr. Bridgwater, Somerset.

THE DANDIE DINMONT TERRIER CLUB OF AMERICA: Dr. M. Josephine Deubler, 2811 Hopkinson House, Washington Square South, Philadelphia, Pennsylvania, 19106.

NOTE: While the addresses given have been checked at the time of proofing this book they cannot be guaranteed as correct indefinitely, owing to the frequent changes in conditions,

A SELECTED BIBLIOGRAPHY

Few of the following books deal purely and simply with the Dandie Dinmont Terrier, and this bibliography could have been extended by the inclusion of the numerous so-called autobiographies, memoirs and other books of sentimental or light literature appertaining to the Dandie Dinmont Terrier, but as they do not contribute materially to a study of the breed they have been omitted from the list.

ASH, E. C.: *Dogs: Their History and Development*, London, 1927.

BEILBY, W.: *The Dog in Australasia*, Melbourne, 1897.

BLAGG, E. W. H.: 'The Dandie Dinmont Terrier' in *Dogs: By Well-Known Authorities*, by Harding Cox, London, 1906.

BROUGHAM, LORD: *Dialogue of Instinct*, 1837.

BROWN, DR. J.: *Horæ Subsecivæ*, Edinburgh, 1858.

BROWN, CAPT. T.: *Biographical Sketches and Authentic Anecdotes of Dogs*, Edinburgh, 1829.

COMPTON, P.: *The Twentieth Century Dog*, London (n.d.).

COOK, C.: *The Dandie Dinmont Terrier*, Edinburgh, 1885.

DALZIEL, H.: *British Dogs*, London, 1879–80.

DANIEL, REV. W. B.: *Rural Sports*, London, 1801–2.

DRURY, W.: *British Dogs*, London, 1903.

GORDON, J. F.: *The Dandie Dinmont Terrier Handbook*, London, 1959.

GRAY, D. J. T.: *The Dogs of Scotland*, Dundee, 1891.

HUBBARD, C. B. L.: *Dogs in Britain*, London, 1948.

Hutchinson's Popular and Illustrated Dog Encyclopaedia, London, 1935.

JOHNS, R.: *Our Friends the Dandie Dinmont and Skye Terriers*, London, 1938.

LANE, C. H.: *Dog Shows and Doggy People*, London, 1902.

LEE, R. B.: *Modern Dogs: The Terrier*, London, 1896.

LEIGHTON, R.: *The New Book of the Dog*, London, 1907; *The Complete Book of the Dog*, London, 1922.

MCCANDLISH, L. L.: 'Dandie Dinmont', in *The Book of the Dog*, edited by Brian Vesey-FitzGerald, London, 1948.

Magazine, The Dandie Dinmont Terrier Club's, Lanark, 1968 *et seq.*

MEYRICK, J.: *House Dogs and Sporting Dogs*, London, 1861.

'REDMARSHALL': *The Bedlington Terrier*, Camberley, 1935.

SHAW, V. K.: *The Illustrated Book of the Dog*, London, 1879–81.

SMITH, A. C.: *About Our Dogs*, London, 1931. *Hounds and Dogs*, London, 1932.

STABLES, A. C.: *Our Friend the Dog*, London (n.d.).

'STONEHENGE': see J. H. Walsh.

The Supplement (breed bulletin edited in the beginning of the present century by Mrs. T. Simpson Shaw).

WALSH, J. H.: *The Dogs of the British Islands*, London, 1867.

WATSON, J.: *The Dog Book*, London, 1906.

WILLIAMS, R. P.: *The Dandie Dinmont Terrier*, London (n.d.).

YOUATT, W.: *The Dog*, London, 1845.

INDEX